THE TAOIST ART

'Hand of the V

An illustrated guide to this unique Chinese system of self-defence which combines 'softness' with speed to great effect.

Other titles in the series

Taoist Arts of the Lee style

by Chee Soo

THE TAO OF MY THOUGHTS

A practical guide to the day to day application of the Taoist philosophy that is the heart of the Lee Style.

ISBN - 0954524454

THE CHINESE ART OF T'AI CHI CH'UAN

The Taoist Way to mental and physical health.

A dynamic aid to health and inner tranquillity through controlled movements for self-defence and the development of physical and mental powers.

ISBN - 0954524403

THE TAO OF LONG LIFE

The Chinese Art of Ch'ang Ming

Health and long life using a time tested approach to diet and nutrition that has been practised by Taoists for thousands of years.

ISBN - 0954524438

THE TAOIST WAYS OF HEALING

The Chinese Art of Pa Chin Hsien

An introduction to the complete system of ancient Chinese Taoist health arts the 'Eight Strands of the Brocade'.

ISBN - 0954524446

THE TAOIST ART OF K'AI MEN

Opening the door to your inner self through Chi Gung

Physical rejuvenation and mental vigour through this ancient and powerful system of energy utilization.

ISBN - 0954524411

THE TAOIST ART OF FENG SHOU

'Hand of the Wind' kung fu

by
CHEE SOO

Seahorse Books
www.seahorsearts.co.uk

Seahorse Books,
www.seahorsearts.co.uk
First published 1983
Second Impression 1984
Third Impression 1986

This edition published by Seahorse Books

Be warned, Feng Shou Kung Fu is not a sport or a game. You should not attempt to learn Kung Fu just by reading a book, make sure you study with a properly qualified teacher. The techniques presented in this manual are for reference purposes only and are for the exclusive use of the members of the Taoist Cultural Arts Association. This work should not be used as a stand alone training tool. The exercises presented herein are completely safe but are specifically designed to be practised exclusively under the direct supervision of a fully qualified teacher in the Lee style of Feng Shou Ch'uan Shu under the Taoist Cultural Arts Association. Anyone practising these exercises without such supervision does so entirely at their own risk, and neither the author nor the publisher nor the Taoist Cultural Arts Association can be held responsible for any damage, financial loss or personal injury to the self or others which may result through the use or mis-use of the techniques shown herein.

Seahorse Books is a part of the
Taoist Cultural Arts Association
Printed and bound in Great Britain by
Creative Print and Design, Ebbw Vale, Wales
Produced using Scribus Open Source software.
http://www.scribus.net

Contents

Acknowledgements

I would like to express my gratitude to Jason Fitzsimmons, Richard Gaston, Avril Grant, Mike Gunn, Steve Hawker, Justin Knight, Sadie Knight, Dan McCarthy, Amanda Morris, Barrie Morris, Asher Simpson, Rachel Simpson and Alex Woolner for the time and help they gave in the preparation of this book. Our deepest gratitude goes to Marilyn Soo for all the help and guidance she has given us over the years and also for giving us the exclusive copyright for this book, and of course to Chee Soo our teacher who made it all possible.

Chris Simpson

Chapter 1

Wu-Shu — Chinese Martial Arts

Feng Shou (Hand of the Wind) style is practised by the Taoist Cultural Arts Association, and it is this particular style that you will be learning in this book. Should you find it of interest, and you would like to learn more about Feng Shou from qualified teachers, then visit our website for the name and the address of your nearest club.

Most of the Chinese styles of kung fu fall into certain easily recognizable groups, and Feng Shou happens to be a very soft, gentle style, which in China we call the Internal Systems (Nei Hsi). Basically, the soft styles use Inner Power (Nei Ch'i) but this is more commonly known to the Taoists as the Vitality Power (Sheng Ch'i), which is generally shortened to Ch'i. Everyone who practises the Taoist arts aims to develop and cultivate Ch'i, for it is absolutely important and essential to the good health of the body, mind and the spirit too.

Don't get the wrong impression about the word 'soft', for Feng Shou is just as lethal as any other style, including the so-called 'hard' styles, but instead of using brute muscular strength to strike with, we use the dynamic force of Ch'i. Also, because it is soft, we have very relaxed movements and the body is constantly in motion with a fast, smooth-flowing action. The majority of the hand and arm movements are mainly circular, sometimes very small, whilst others can be very big rotary actions.

If you practise everything in this book, and attain a certain degree of perfection in each movement, don't think that you will then know the whole art of Feng Shou. You will be very wrong, for you will have only just got through the beginners' class, so you are still a comparative novice. For instance, look at the number of Foot Patterns in this book; when you realize that we have a total of 131 foot techniques in all, you will appreciate that you are just beginning to scratch the surface of this dynamic art. So take your time, practise and keep on practising at every opportunity, for only constant practise can lead you to the realm of perfection. That is our main objective and we still wonder if we will ever attain it in our lifetime, but we keep trying. Having spent over forty-five years in this art, we realize now, more than ever, that it will take a lifetime to perfect it and reach the standard that we personally would like to achieve. We truly wonder if we will ever reach the ultimate objective, but we still keep trying and training, and after all these years we shall certainly not give up now.

Many of the famous masters of ancient China were very particular about who they should pass their knowledge of the arts on to, and they therefore put every one of their pupils through very strict training schedules. These lasted for very long periods, until that pupil had truly proved himself to be not only dedicated, but also worthy of carrying on the secrets of the art to others, and that he had the loyalty and the capacity to work really hard. There were no gradings in those far-off days so the only way a pupil could become a teacher was when his own master thought he was ready to take on that responsibility, and had proved himself over and over again in every way.

Our own master, Chan Kam Lee, the founder of the International Wu-Shu Association, was no exception, and his principles were impressed upon us to such a degree that we have been reluctant to pass on further knowledge until a pupil had proved himself truly worthy. That is why we helped to set up the International Coaching Centres in 1958, so that all prospective teachers and coaches could seriously get down to the hard and gritty task of strenuously learning all the fundamental basics necessary for teachers to pass on to their own students. They learn the basic art of how to teach others and how to instruct new techniques. They learn how to maintain harmony within a class (especially where there is a mixture of age groups and sexes) and how to hold the interest of the students (which is not the easiest of tasks, even with experienced pupils). It isn't everyone who can become a really good teacher, even though they might have the knowledge and the skill.

However, the old masters were never confronted with the same situation that everyone finds himself in today. For one thing, no one can dedicate himself to the arts twenty-four hours a day, seven days a week, and live his life entirely with the arts, day in and day out; everyone has to earn a living, and therefore it is only in his spare time that the enthusiast can follow his interest. If his local club can only open once or twice a week, then again he is unable to express his innermost dedication. How is it possible to learn all those intricate movements and techniques if you are restricted through your work or the hours of your local club? Some people may be handicapped because they live too far away from a club which practises this art.

So it has become necessary to publish a reliable book or sequence of books that will help everyone in these circumstances and which will stand them in good stead, at all times. It will also give them a reference to any technical points which have been forgotten over a long period of time, or which have been overlooked during an interruption of the training. This is also why the Taoist Cultural Arts Association endeavours to run regular coaching classes in various parts of the world.

The true style of Feng Shou is taught and practised only in the Taoist Cultural Arts Association and it is only this Association that still faithfully passes on the true Taoist techniques and adheres to the same standards that have been passed down through the generations of Taoist teachers to the present day.

It is the stringent adherence to the basic foundations that were laid down by the Lee family of Wei Hei Wei, central China, that has kept this style as pure today as it was when it was formulated over 2,000 years ago.

All teachers within the Association teach exactly the same techniques for each of the grading standards, so Feng Shou can not become the kind of bastard style that so many other styles have turned into. This has happened because some teachers in those styles have deviated in their teaching, and so over a period of time that style has changed from the one originally formulated by the masters of old, and now many of the very foundations of the art no longer exist. This is a great shame, for the old masters put a lifetime of work, dedication and experience into making them what they were, and to have the styles altered by others who do not have the same experience means that somewhere along the way many essentials and basics have become lost.

Although there are a million 'secrets' within our art, we are not going to make any boasts that we can give any away, for the understanding of many of these can only come through actual practise with qualified teachers, who can show you some of these practically and personally. It is impossible to put them down on paper. The realization of other secrets comes with feeling, intuition, direction, mental control, experience and many from spiritual growth, and you alone can only find them for they are very personal to you. You will be helped by little knacks that you acquire and the feel of a certain technique — whilst you might seem to do it exactly the same way as everyone else, by putting your own personality behind it and within it, it becomes an integral part of yourself. You have to go through this alone for they are all a part of your experience, and only time can give you that wealth.

In that respect, these so-called secrets are common knowledge to all, providing we persevere in our training. Some are relatively simple to master, but others take a long time and they will only come with time, practise and perseverance.

Your Inner Power is the doorway through which all are equal as this depends entirely on your development of the natural internal power, and not on the size of your muscles. Hence even the smallest and the weakest men and women can fully defend themselves against the tall and the strong.

Of course, there are other factors that must be taken into consideration, for instance: the ability to use the right technique at the right time, and spontaneously as well as correctly, if you are attacked; the sense of touch that enables you to feel and exploit an opponent's lack of adequate balance; the skill and ability to use blind blows, which are ones that your opponent will certainly feel, but will never see, even if you are standing directly in front of him; the intuition and sixth sense through which you can tell when and how your opponent will attack, even though you may not be able to see him.

Inner Power is something you should 'feel' as you progress through the arts, although it may not become apparent for possibly twelve months or more. Using the correct technique at the precise moment when the weakness or opportunity presents itself will become second nature to you over a period of time, and it is entirely dependent on the amount of practise that you are able to put in. This also applies to acquiring the feel of balance.

The intention of this book is therefore to try to give you a basic knowledge of the stances, foot work, hand techniques and body movements that are the foundation of Feng Shou, our style of kung fu.

We have included the equivalent Chinese terminology for the various moves, stances etc., in Mandarin, since this is the most widely spoken dialect in China, and it is now becoming the national and universal language.

Many of the techniques in this book can be practised alone, but you will need the help of a partner when you come to the more complicated moves, so try and find a friend to practise with who is as interested in the art as you are. Women and men can practise this art together easily, and more than a third of the membership of the Association are women.

Don't forget to practise constantly and diligently, and you will eventually master these basic techniques and movements and reach quite a high standard of proficiency.

Chapter 2

The History of Kung Fu

No one can say exactly when the Chinese arts of self-defence first came into being, but the seeds go back to the very early days of the primitive period, when man first roamed the earth. Before he had even invented a weapon, man had to protect himself with his bare hands against the attacks of his fellow countrymen as well as the wild animals.

So this man and beast situation existed throughout the primitive world: sooner or later it had to come to be that one or the other species had to assert its overall mastery and supremacy, and it was then that the Chinese really excelled, and laid down the foundations for all humanity to follow. Once they had learnt to master themselves, and anything that threatened their existence, and learnt to organize their family groups, they went on to build the earliest civilizations in that period. The techniques and the knowledge that they used eventually spread way beyond their boundaries and shores, and helped many other people and races in far-off territories.

Not only did the Chinese excel in all aspects of silk weaving, gunpowder making, painting, building wells and irrigation systems, herbal therapy, and all the other dynamic health arts including Ch'ang Ming, through the great wisdom and knowledge brought to them by the 'Sons of Reflected Light', but they were the first nation to put martial arts on a scientific basis. This was because not only did they explore every avenue of physical dexterity and manipulation, but they also used the natural dynamic vitality power of the body (Sheng Ch'i) and the enormous macro-cosmic power of the universe (Ching Sheng Li), and these are still being used by the Chinese through the Taoist Arts, and in Feng Shou which is our particular style of kung fu.

Kung fu, means 'working man' or 'man of the fist' depending

on the way it is written in Chinese, and we shall devote ourselves to this, and to the understanding of its origins.

We know that the fighting styles used by many Oriental countries, including the Japanese Karate and the Korean art of Tae Kwan Do, are adaptions and imitations of the basic forms of various styles of kung fu, taught to the local inhabitants by Chinese immigrants, and which were eventually adapted to suit the needs and attitudes of these lands.

Some of the various styles that have evolved have changed to such a degree that in many cases they no longer bear the slightest resemblance to the original foundation given by the Chinese, and so it is not surprising that many followers of these newer arts try to forget that they owe their skills to the early Chinese, and overlook the close links that these arts once had. Within China the original kung fu foundations were laid down in the primitive period, as we have already mentioned, but the actual records of the arts only go back some 5,000 years.

One of the main reasons why there is so little information available on the early days of the martial arts, is because none of the early masters or their pupils kept precise written records of their training programmes or the techniques that they practised. This was due, no doubt, to the fact that this information was not intended for the general public, but only for those pupils who proved themselves worthy of the techniques, skills and the tradition of that particular school or style. So, generally, these were closely-guarded secrets, and were handed down from father to son, master to pupil, and generation to generation.

When the student also became a master, in his own right, he too would only pass on his skills and knowledge to those he thought would not only be worthy of them, but who would also treasure them as he had done over many, many years. In fact, the knowledge of the art of 'Feng Shou' goes back at least 2,000 years, and has been handed down through the Lee family for all this time, and has been passed to us by our late master, Chan Kam Lee. Add the modesty and the humility that are impressed upon every Chinese child, and the philosophy that is inbred in his daily life, and you can perhaps understand why so few records were ever kept.

Yet despite this, we know that a brilliant doctor called Hwa T'or formulated a series of movements coupled with special breathing exercises that were intended to limber up the body, ease the nerves, and generally reduce bodily tensions. We also know that the Taoists formulated many specialized stances and exercises together with many precise breathing formulas in K'ai Men (the Open Door) which is the Taoist Yoga, and in T'ai Chi Ch'uan (the Supreme Ultimate) in their long search for physical alchemy.

All these have been so successful that they are still in use today, although over the centuries certain modifications have quite naturally taken place. Many of the breathing exercises are practised in the Chinese Health Arts of Pa Chin Hsien (Eight Strands of the Brocade) where they help to effect many cures for a large variety of ailments and sickness. They are also the basic foundation for the development, cultivation, activation, of the Internal Energy (Sheng Ch'i) and the External Energy (Ching Sheng Li).

According to tradition, after the Taoists and Hwa T'or laid down the early foundations, there came a Buddhist monk called Bodhiharma, who, in 500 AD left his Brahman tribe in southern India and crossed the Himalayas into China. After a long, slow and laborious journey across extremely rugged terrain, he eventually arrived at Chien K'ang, which was then the capital of the Liang province.

It was well known that the Emperor Wu was a Buddhist with an enthusiastic interest in all Buddhist doctrines. On learning this, Bodhiharma immediately sought an audience with the Emperor, and as a result the monk was given permission to teach and preach in the province.

So Bodhidharma began spreading the word and the doctrine of Ch'an, which the Japanese later adapted and called Zen. However, at that time it was found that these teachings not only clashed with the beliefs and the philosophy of the Chinese, but they were also found to be so complex that everyone, including the Emperor, found it extremely difficult to grasp even the fundamentals. This therefore created a tremendous amount of friction, frustration, irritation, and eventually such bad feeling towards Bodhiharma that he was dismissed from the Emperor's service.

It was then that he decided to travel northwards, although nobody knows why he decided to take that particularly difficult direction. The roads were extremely bad and in some cases almost non-existent, and he spoke very little Chinese so there was also a language problem, made worse by the fact that there would have been many different dialects spoken on this long journey. A greater hazard was the many roaming armed bands of thieves and robbers in the countryside along his chosen route. Small wonder then that it took him more than three years to cross the Yangtse River, and reach his intended destination of the Shaolin Temple at Sung Shan in Henan province.

He stayed at the Shaolin Temple for nearly ten years, teaching and meditating, and it was during the latter part of his stay that he realized that many of his pupils were not fit enough, either mentally or physically, to endure the physical austerity imposed by his teachings.

Ch'an Buddhism was based on very deep meditation with its aims being the unification of mind, body and spirit, and therefore Bodhiharma felt that physical endurance would help to equip his pupils for this objective. He borrowed a number of the Taoist stances and exercises, and hardened them up to create within the practitioners a sense of internal strength, and a feeling of inseparability of mind and spirit within the body. Thus he encouraged literally throwing yourself within yourself, becoming one single entity with all three parts becoming one, and so achieving constant harmony in the daily toil of life.

Many of these exercises would not be classed as entirely physical by today's standards, especially as the feet made no movement at all; even so, they soon earned the Shaolin monks the reputation of being China's toughest and the most formidable unarmed fighters.

Strangely enough, though, despite the monastery's nationwide reputation, Bodhiharma's pupils gradually dwindled away. This may have been due to the complexity and the severity of his teachings. However, part of his work and the foundation that he laid down still lived on, and to those basic exercises and movements, others were gradually added and further techniques evolved and so kung fu in its earliest form came into being.

It has been established that Bodhiharma did actually exist during this period, but how much he actually contributed to the art of kung fu, as we know it today, will always remain a controversial subject. But there is no doubt whatsoever, that he did lay the foundation on which are built many of the hard styles and solid defensive systems of the art of the Chinese boxing art of kung fu.

Another very significant period in the history of this art was the Sung Dynasty (960-1279) which brought about a radical change in Chinese thinking which gradually affected not only kung fu but all the arts. Until this time, the techniques were carried out from very stiff and static stances, in an endeavour to harden and toughen the body which in those days was considered essential to any martial art practitioner, together with synchronized movements and the use of sheer brute muscular strength. Indeed, many martial art schools still teach this style, and the Japanese Karate is based on these same principles.

But the really important change came about when stiffness was replaced by pliability, static techniques were overcome with speed and dexterity, and internal or intrinsic energy took the place of physical and muscular strength.

From this time onwards, the Chinese arts made fantastic progress, and the technical advancement was so progressive that even the old masters of the arts were amazed. Since those early days many famous Chinese have made their mark on the martial arts by adding techniques, new adaptations, new systems of exercising and training, new forms and sets of movements, and have, in some cases, made improvements on the old techniques.

By reducing the necessity of using muscular strength, the arts then became available even to the very young and the very old alike, and girls and women could now participate as well.

To this day there are many Chinese schools and hospitals who use the classic sets of movements (especially T'ai Chi Ch'uan), as a form of physical therapy. But it is not limited to this alone, for in modern China it is a common sight to see groups of people, men and women, getting together during the factory or office lunch break and performing some of these sets, simply to control the mind, to keep the body fit, and to attain internal peace and tranquillity.

China is a massive country and, like all countries, in the old days the communications were very poor, and just as dialects occurred in the national language, so did variations and differences appear in the styles of kung fu.

Furthermore, those Chinese who emigrated in the past to other countries took their own particular style of kung fu with them, and its evolution was largely independent of Chinese thought. So in places like Hong Kong, Malaya, Hawaii, California, and other areas where there are large gatherings of Chinese, there are a number of schools, each with its own methods and systems of training.

The main difference that stamps a particular style is the use of the hands and their adaptions and, to a lesser degree, the use of the feet — except in the very northern schools where the feet are used to a far greater extent.

The environment has played the most important part in the establishment of styles, and even to some extent the various techniques that were used. In the south where there were large open spaces of paddy fields, swamps and jungle bogs, and where large fishing fleets sailed around the coast, then hand techniques had to be used more because the legs were either soaked in mud and water up to the knees, or the feet were necessary to retain good balance whilst on board a boat rocking on the high seas. In the mountains of the north, the ground was hard, thus allowing greater flexibility in the use of the foot and leg techniques.

There are still many styles existing in the world today, and these are normally defined under certain categories, such as the 'soft' style (Juan Shou), 'hard fist' style (Ying Ch'uan), 'short' style (Tuan), 'long' style (Ch'ang), 'hand art' (Shou Shu) and the 'foot art' (Jiao Shu).

The Feng Shou (pronounced in Mandarin as 'Fung Show') style of kung fu that we practise in the Taoist Cultural Arts Association consists of a complete mixture of all the above categories, because the style emanated from Central China, and therefore had the advantage of using the best from both the southern and northern styles, so it has everything in it, together with its own unique dynamic style. It is basically a 'soft' style, which means that we use speed, skill, wonderful balance, and we build up our Inner Power to such an advanced degree that we have no need whatsoever to use our physical or muscular strength. We are the softest and fastest style in existence.

In the Chinese arts we will never say that one style is better than another because all Chinese admire one another and will do all they can to help and assist each other whenever required. However, it must be understood that if you rely on pure physical strength, then you can be defeated by a much stronger opponent, providing, of course, the standard of skill is equal. In the soft arts we do not use physical strength so we do not have to rely upon it, and therefore it is skill that counts, plus the use of internal power which has to be developed to such a degree that it will be far superior to any form of physical strength anyway.

Whilst many of the styles today emanated from the earliest teachings of Ch'an Buddhism at the Shaolin Temple, our particular style of Feng Shou goes back much earlier in time, in fact, to the very early formation of exercising by the Taoists, and our Taoism unites all of us in the Taoist Cultural Arts Association in our aims, ideals, and our physical path together with our spiritual growth.

We are one within the Taoists arts, and we are one with our Maker.

Chapter 3

Etiquette

The Chinese have always had a great respect for their elders in the family and within the community, and this external sign of courtesy and homage was symbolized in the kung fu schools and clubs in a variety of different ways. These expressions were through an outward sign of hand, body and foot movements, and in some instances a combination of two or even the entire use of all three, depending on the particular meaning that the club or school wished to convey, and generally known only to the members of the school or club concerned.

The sign of respect that is used in the Taoist Cultural Arts Association is nearly 2,000 years old, and was originally devised by the Lee family, and has been handed down through their family ever since. It is used at the beginning and the end of every training session, and it consists of an open right hand, with the palm facing downward, placed on top of a clenched left fist, which is held close to the waistline on the left side of the body.

As soon as the hands reach their allotted positions, the left foot steps back one pace, followed by the right foot, so both feet are once more level with one another and close together.

Both hands are then brought to the front of the body, and the left wrist is gripped by the right hand, and the right wrist is gripped by the left hand. As soon as this is completed, the body is bent forward to about an angle of ninety degrees, and as the head will move with the body, the nape of the neck is shown. This is an act of trust and faith that you will not be attacked whilst you are performing your salutation.

This is our formal salutation, which has five meanings, based on the five element principle of the universe:

1. We will always respect the illustrious founder of our system, all those who have studied with him, and all those who have studied and practised his arts.
2. We humbly pay homage and respect to our present teacher.
3. We respect all students and masters who study the national arts and crafts of China.
4. We practise in complete friendship, and will not attack you unexpectedly. We therefore hide our fist as a sign of our goodwill.
5. We shall always remain humble, and promise never to misuse the skill or the knowledge that has been given to us.

The hiding of the left fist under the open right hand, is a sign that the fist has not seen the light, and thus it is a token of self humility. The open right hand is the progression of one over another, and it represents softness which will always be superior to hardness. It is also a sign of the Yin and Yang, which denotes the balance within everything that exists, and the supreme harmony according to the universal laws of the TAO (Way).

The closed fist denotes contraction and as it is the left that is clenched, they both represent the Yin aspect. The open right hand is Yang, and the open hand shows natural expansion which is also Yang. To those who practise Feng Shou it also has a further meaning, for it shows the recall (Yin) and the dynamic expression (Yang) of Ch'i energy, and lets your partner know that you will not even use your intrinsic energy against him, while you are bowing to him, for by this open sign you show him that you have closed your upper circuit.

The right arm sweeping across the front of the body also shows homage and deep respect, and that you cannot use any weapon that may be hidden up the sleeves, and stepping backward, in so doing increasing the distance between the two parties, shows trust and friendship. The bending of the body reflects your humble disposition, and the willingness to learn without the misuse of the arts.

The Personal Salutation is used when you are about to practise with another person, or have finished your session with him, whereupon you place your left fist into the palm of your right hand, and, holding both hands in front of your chest, bow

the head and shoulders about forty-five degrees. This not only denotes your personal respect for the person you are going to practise with, and trust and homage that you feel towards him, but again it is another sign of the Yin and Yang, and everything that they convey.

The Homage Salutation is a sign of homage and respect and is used when you enter or leave the practice room (Ts'ao Fang). It is also used when you arrive after the class has commenced: then it is common courtesy and a part of our etiquette to make your salutation to the master or teacher in charge, and ask permission to join the class, and you salute again to him if he grants permission to you. This salutation is performed by the simple process of standing with your feet together, and placing both open hands on the front of your own thighs. This is another way of showing that you are unarmed and that you wish to show your goodwill and trust. You then bow the head and shoulders to about forty-five degrees with your eyes looking down to the floor. This shows self humility, homage and respect to your teacher and to everyone who has practised or will practise in the room. This same procedure must also be followed if you want to leave the class, during the lesson, for some reason or another.

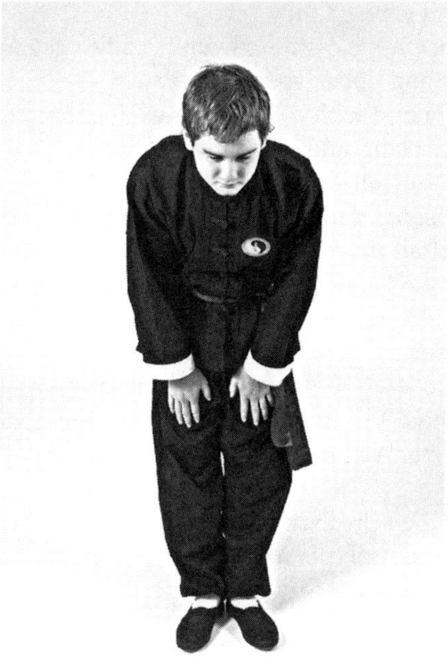

Humility, courtesy and respect is always shown to all masters, whether you are in a practice room or outside in the street, for this is the first lesson of all practitioners of the arts, in the attainment of self discipline and complete self control.

Our President is therefore always referred to as 'Lao Fu' (Old Father) which in China is a very sincere greeting of respect. All other masters and teachers in the arts are referred to as 'Hsien Sheng' (Teacher).

At all times the student must try to emulate the true spirit of the Knights of ancient China, and strictly adhere to the code of honour of the Taoist Cultural Arts Association that was originally laid down by the Lee family, and brought to us by Chan Kam Lee.

In 1931 Chan Kam Lee formulated the eight golden rules that we live by, practise, and endeavour to uphold at all times, and these are:

1. Lead a clean and pure life in mind, body and spirit, and always follow the WAY of the TAO.
2. Obey your instructor at all times and do so without question.
3. Control your mind first, your spirit second, and your body third.
4. Before you try to understand other people, first learn to understand yourself fully.
5. Never use physical strength under any circumstances. Learn to acquire and utilize your Inner Power.
6. Always practise with a feeling of exhilaration, but ensure that you practise hard and diligently.
7. The Chinese self-defence arts must only be used when you are in personal danger, or if you should see someone else in danger. At all times, if trouble confronts you, use every effort to settle the matter peaceably. If that fails, then, and only then, should you use the arts, but in any case, they should be used only as the very last resort.
8. Follow the example as set by your own master, and at all times uphold the honour, dignity, and the good name of the International Wu Shu Association.

Etiquette and the self-discipline of oneself is the first step towards the complete control of yourself, which helps in moments of stress, but also aids your training, especially when moving at very high speeds, when reaction has to be instantaneous, and counterattacks have to be automatic. It is then when full mind control harmonized with the body will come out in full bloom.

Chapter 4

Clothing

If you are going to participate in this art, or even practise at home, you will certainly want to be comfortable, and be able to move around easily without being restricted by your clothing. So this is something that you will have to think about before you start your training.

Most of the clubs and schools that teach kung fu in the West use Judo or Karate suits, and practise in their bare feet to try and harden the soles of their feet. The authentic kung fu clubs will buy their requirements from Hong Kong, and whilst they look very nice they do have a tendency to stick to the skin because they are generally made from silk, nylon or rayon fabrics, so are a bit uncomfortable when you perspire.

However, our Association has its own specially-made uniform, which you can see from the illustrations, it is based on the design of traditonal chinese clothing for Taoist martial Arts. It is made of cotton, which is light and allows a current of air to circulate round the inside of the jacket so that it is very cool to work in, and being loose it does not restrict the very fast movements that are required in our art. Another important aspect is the colour of our suits which has foundations going back many thousands of years into Chinese mythology.

As you have read, our Chinese boxing style is known as Feng Shou, meaning 'Hand of the Wind', and this has its connection with the 'Earl of the Wind' whose name was Feng Po. Now in Chinese mythology he is depicted as a very old man with a long flowing white beard, who stands on the green grass of the heavens' highest pinnacle, dressed in a yellow cloak and wearing a red and blue hat. In his hands he holds the open end of a cotton sack, and wherever he points the mouth of the sack, so the wind blows in that direction.

Thus from his exalted position in the heavens he can turn a

full circle, and send the winds unhindered across the whole world. If he moves slowly then the wind from the sack will hardly move, so it will feel like the gentleness of a morning breeze, but if he becomes angry or is surprised then he may turn very fast, and the wind will hurtle across the universe to become and create the devastation of a tornado. So don't upset him by becoming aggressive for the one thing he really hates is violence.

No matter what force he may use at any time, you will never see it, although you will see the results of it or its after-effects, like the leaves being tossed around or the grass bending over. In his more serious moods, you may see the roots of a tree being pulled out of the ground, or roofs being torn off houses, or even ships being tossed onto the land as if they were match sticks.

He never gives his intentions away so you can never anticipate his actions and as you can never see him, you never know if he is near you or not. So it is with our Hand of the Wind style of kung fu.

In all, there are seven arts based on the mythology of Feng Po, and the same standard of grading applies in each one, no matter which art you might be studying. The rank of each participant is denoted by the colour of the sashes or belts worn by the Teachers or Masters, and here the colours of Feng Po are used, in accordance with the standard of grade that has been obtained.

However, there is one exception to all these colours which is white and black, which shows that the wearer has reached the stage of occlusion and the harmony of the Yin and Yang.

If you are practising at home it is not essential to have our uniform, but if you do join one of the many clubs within our organization then, of course, it will be necessary to have a proper suit. An instructor will be able to inform you about this when the time comes. For the time being, make use of what you have in your wardrobe, but ensure that it is loose-fitting, so don't wear tight jeans; you will find that some light-weight plimsolls will be ideal for your feet, and a T-shirt should complete your practice attire.

Of course, this is only for use during practice, for once you have acquired a high standard of skill, it does not matter what you might be wearing, for you will still be able to look after yourself.

If the occasion should ever arise, and let us hope that it never will, you will be just as good in a three-piece suit, a boiler suit, or even in your birthday suit. That will show you the adaptability of your nature and your mind within the arts.

Chapter 5

Limbering Exercises

Mention exercises to anyone and they will immediately think of press-ups and the monotony of trying to build up big muscles and strong physical strength. This is not so in the art of Feng Shou, where lightness, dexterity and speed are the main requirements; this is stressed to all the students who take up our art.

Our exercises were never designed as muscle-building callisthenics, for their main object is to keep very soft and supple, and to loosen the entire body in such a way as to keep the muscular system relaxed at all times. Naturally, being physically fit is essential in all types of physical activity, but it is more so in Feng Shou where high speeds, fast evasions, quick ward-offs, and split second reactions are so necessary to evade sudden and unexpected attacks. Obviously someone who is physically fit and healthy will be quicker on the move than someone who is unfit, in the same way that someone who is fresh and alert is faster than a person who is tired.

So the ultimate results of these exercises will be that you acquire very fast speeds in movement and reactions, possibly increasing your speed by only fractions of a second, but in this art where height, reach, weight and muscular power creates no undue problems, then a split second can make all the difference between success or failure. Anyone who wishes to dedicate themselves to this art, should also learn to live on the 'Ch'ang Ming' (Taoist Long Life) health diet therapy, which ensures that good health internally is constant, and sickness is a thing of the past. In these Taoist arts we have a saying: 'If you lose your temper once in a lifetime - then your mind is sick. If you catch a cold once in a lifetime - then your body is sick. If you catch cancer -then your spirit is sick.' So to ensure that you are constantly healthy, and can obtain the maximum benefit from our arts then eat the Ch'ang Ming way, the sensible eating and drinking habits of the Taoists.

We realize, especially after a hard day's work, that you might consider exercising as an unnecessary tedious chore, and something you will be tempted to bypass. This is largely due to the fact that in the past all forms of exercising have been forced upon you, and were something that you did not want to do anyway. Once you start our limbering movements, and do them regularly every day, you will alter your attitudes because you will feel the difference that good health can bring.

Remember, we are not going to force you to do them - no way! You can please yourself, but if you are left standing still by someone who is literally walking rings around you, and your reactions are so slow, you cannot even ward off his blow, then you may perhaps realize the disadvantages of not keeping yourself healthy and fit.

Try them out, and put some effort in doing them, and get into the right spirit from the start, and after a while you will realize how important they are to your rate of progress. If you haven't taken much exercise recently then start off a little slowly and in a few days you will be able to go right through the recommended number of repetitions without any undue exertion or strain.

Physical fitness helps you to develop in many ways, and not only the physical side of your life: it helps the co-ordination of balance, gives you greater perception so that you can feel danger even before it becomes obvious, it develops your intuition so that you have greater understanding and appreciation of any situation that may arise, and it opens up the whole body so that your Inner Power can not only be developed, but will open up the various channels so necessary for the Ch'i to be able to flow freely. All exercises that are included in Feng Shou are designed to help you along this road. So enjoy them and practise them at least once a day, and the best time is, naturally, at the beginning of your training session.

Sitting and Lying Exercises

1. *Ankle Rolling*

Sit on the floor with your left leg straight, bend your right knee and cross your right ankle over your left leg so that it rests just above the left knee. Grip the toes of your right foot with your left hand, and hold your right ankle with your right hand. Now rotate the foot round in big circles, about twelve times. Now place the right leg back on to the floor, and cross the left leg over the right and repeat the sequence, but this time gripping your left toes with your right hand, and then rotating the ankle about twelve times.

This will loosen off the joints of the ankle, and is very necessary, especially in cold weather. Remember that the ankle and the knee take the weight of the body all the time, and so it is important to have strong yet supple ankles, and this exercise will give them the benefit that they need and deserve.

2. Head Bending

Whilst sitting on the floor keep your right leg straight, and bend the left leg back so that the left foot is placed to the rear beyond your left hip. Now grip your right ankle or foot with your right hand and the shin of your left leg with the left hand, and try and place your forehead onto your right knee, without bending your right leg. Six times will be enough, but each time straighten the body before bending down again. Change legs and repeat another six times by bending down towards your left knee.

3. Shoulder Cycling

Lie flat on your back and raise both legs into the air, so that the weight of your body is on your shoulders, and as you do so, support your back with your hands, using your elbows to make a tripod on the floor. Now rotate your legs in really big circles, just as if you were cycling, starting very slowly at first, then slowly increasing the speed until the last few rotations are done as fast as you can. About twenty revolutions of the legs should be sufficient.

4. Leg Swinging

While you are lying on your back with your legs out straight, and keeping them both together, swing them directly over your head, trying to touch the floor with the toes of both feet. Then let the legs swing back lightly to the floor, as you were when you first started. Now swing your legs into the air once more, but this time instead of taking them over the head, swing them over your left shoulder till the toes touch the floor once again. Then return to your starting position. Now repeat this sequence by swinging the legs over the right shoulder, touching the floor with the toes, and returning to the starting position. Three to five sets of the full sequence should be sufficient.

5. The Tortoise

Still lying on your back, bend both knees so that the heels of both feet nearly touch your own bottom. Both hands should circle over your own shoulders to a position by the side of your head, with the palms of both hands flat on the floor, fingers pointing towards the ankles. Now push your tummy into the air so that you hollow the back, and allow the head to tilt backwards at the same time. This exercise is really dynamic so take it easy for the first few times, and after a week you should be able to work up to four or six full sequences at each session.

6. Deep Breathing

At this point sit cross-legged on the floor and learn to relax the whole body by letting the shoulders droop downwards, although try and keep the spine upright. Now breathe by taking a deep breath in through the nose and then exhale out through the mouth. Try to breathe through the lower stomach (Tan T'ien), which is technically known as diaphragmatic breathing - in other words, very deep breathing - and concentrate on your lower stomach all the time so that you can feel the tummy going in and out when you inhale and exhale. To give you added proficiency in your early attempts to do this exercise, place both hands on your tummy, so that when you inhale your hands will get pushed outwards, but when you exhale through the mouth, press your tummy strongly with both hands, thereby helping to force out the stale air.

This is just one of the many Taoist breathing exercises that is incorporated in our art, and it is a Yang breathing exercise. You will find that your whole body will have the tendency to warm up quite intensely, it will also aid your concentration, and will keep you very relaxed; in addition, you will find your health improving as more and more oxygen goes into the blood stream. Your energies will also become stronger and you will start to activate your Internal Energy (Ch'i) by constant use of this simple exercise.

When you feel a little listless or tired, or you are under a period of strain or stress, then utilize this deep breathing sequence, and you will find that you obtain great benefit from it.

Now stand up on your feet, and continue with a few more limbering exercises.

Standing Exercises

7. Head Rolling

Drop your head downwards towards your chest and circle it out to your right, then take it backwards, then continue to circle it towards your left shoulder, and then finally back to your front, so that your chin rests once more on to your chest. Now raise the head so that you look directly ahead once more. Now, drop your head forward so your chin touches the chest again, but this time roll the head towards the left shoulder, then backwards so that you look up to the ceiling, then turn it towards your right shoulder, and then once more come back to the centre of the chest. Then raise your head once more so that you look directly ahead. Repeat this sequence three times in each direction.

8. Head Turning

Turn your head sharply to the right, then snap it back so you face to the front, now snap the head sharply to the left, then snap it back to the starting position. Repeat this sequence three times.

9. Head Bend and Raise

Bend your head downward until your chin digs into your chest, then raise the head and tilt it backwards as far as you can without leaning. Then raise your head so that you are looking directly forward once more. Repeat this full sequence five more times, and try to get the maximum extension in both directions.

10. Arm Swinging

With your arms hanging at your thighs, swing your body as far round to your left as you can, letting the arms swing out as you turn. Now swing your whole body around fully to the right, letting your arms follow the natural movement of the body. Execute this simple exercise about twelve times, keeping relaxed as you swing round as far as you can without moving the feet.

11. Hip Rolling

Put your hands on your hips, and roll the hips round in as big a circle as you can possibly manage. First circle it out to your right then all the way round until you come back to the front. Then reverse the movement and swing the hips round to the left in a big circle until you come back to your starting position. Repeat this circular sequence both ways another five times.

12. Side Bending

Swing your left arm directly over your head, and at the same time bend the body deeply sideways to your right. Straighten the body, dropping your left arm to the side of your left hip. Now take your right arm over the head and bend deeply to the left, then straighten the body once more, dropping your right arm down by your right side. Repeat this sequence six times both ways.

13. Arm Pulling

Extend your arms directly in front of the shoulders, then close both hands into tight fists, and pull both arms back sharply towards yourself, so that the knuckles of both fists touch the sides of the chest, just in front of the armpits. At the same time, allow the elbows to go back as far as you can as well. Now open your hands and push your arms directly forward on a line with the shoulders with your fingers pointing straight forward. Practise this series of movements about six times.

14. Chicken Drop

With your feet about the width of your shoulders apart, turn the whole of your body, together with your legs and feet, to your left, and bend your right knee very deeply towards the floor, until it is about one inch from the surface. Now straighten both legs, stand upright, and turn 180° to the right, and this time bend your left knee down towards the floor. Straighten both legs, turn to your left until you are back in your original starting position. That is one set of movements: now repeat the whole sequence, to the left and to the right, another five times.

15. Front Leg Swing

To start this exercise raise your right hand up to the front so that it is on a level with your shoulders, then swing your right foot up to it, until you touch the palm of the hand with your right toes. Now let the leg swing down and back to the starting position, and at the same time lower your right hand alongside your thigh. Now raise the left hand in front of your left shoulder, and swing your left foot up to it till the toes touch your left palm. Then lower the leg and left arm back to their starting positions. Repeat twelve times on each leg. As the legs become more flexible, you can of course, raise your hands higher into the air, so that your kicks become more and more extended, but don't drop your hand down to meet the feet. Remember that you always take the foot up to the palm of each hand, then you will gain the maximum benefit from this exercise.

There is a more difficult way of executing this exercise, once you have obtained the flexibility and control of your legs. You swing your leg into the air first so that it reaches its maximum height, or any height that you choose to take it, then hold it for a fraction of a second in that position, whilst you shoot your hand forward to touch the toes with the palm of the hand, just like Asher is about to do in the picture. All the time you keep your leg straight by ensuring that your knee is kept locked.

16. Leg Sideways

Raise your right leg into the air so that the weight of your body is fully supported on your left leg. Now take your right leg out sideways from the body, straightening the leg as you do so, and make sure that you lock the knee. Hold it in that position for two or three seconds then bend the knee and lower the right leg back to your starting position. Now repeat the same action with your left leg. Six times to the right and six times to the left is enough for this exercise.

17. Leg Backwards

Repeat as in No. 15, but instead of taking the leg sideways, you now take the leg directly backwards, leading with the heel of the foot, and again ensure that you lock the knee and keep the leg absolutely straight. Hold it for a few seconds as you straighten the leg, then lower it back to the floor. Now repeat on the other leg. Again six times on each leg is a nice minimum number, which you should be able to do without too much strain.

As you progress in the practice of the last two exercises and your legs become more and more flexible, you can endeavour to raise your leg higher and higher, so that you get the maximum benefit from the muscle changes that take place.

Of course, if you have not done any exercises for some time, you are bound to feel the effects at first, so after your first few evenings' exercising, jump into a nice warm bath and lie in it for a little while, and this will ease the stiffness away. But in any case, for the first week or so, take it nice and easy, to allow the body time to tune up, and you will find that you do not become too stiff at the beginning of your training, so you will become more relaxed and more supple a little quicker. None of the exercises are too strenuous, and they were never intended to be so, for they are purely designed to keep the muscles soft, then to make them more supple and flexible, that is why they are purely limbering exercises.

Big muscles are something that you do not want, and neither do you need, for in the soft arts of China and especially in our style of Feng Shou, big muscles is a sign, and a sure sign, of ill health and internal weakness. Through our gentle exercises you will open up the channels within the body, and thereby you will find that your Inner Power (Ch'i) will slowly get stronger and stronger, and it will also be able to flow that much more freely and easily. Hardness and tension will restrict the channels, even close them up in some cases, so that the Ch'i cannot flow at all, or only dribbles along those restricted channels.

With the easy and constant flow of Ch'i also comes good health together with a stronger mind; the more easily it flows the greater the development of your internal energy, so much so that eventually you could have the same power as six men without using a single ounce of physical strength.

Chapter 6

Stances

Whether you are standing or walking, or even if you happen to lean sideways you are in one of the natural stances of our Chinese arts. Such stances are used, not only to combine the balance of the body to a perfection, but to harmonize it with movement so that you can retain speed, subtlety from one posture to another and still remain completely in charge of the situation and have control of yourself at all times.

Most people do not realize how weak the human body really is. No matter how you stand you will always have six points of weakness, and therefore can be easily moved, tugged, pushed or lifted in all directions very, very simply, even with the pressure of one finger. It is this that makes correct stances a very important and an integral part of your kung fu training. You must be able to stand, move forward, sideways, backwards, rotate, walk, jump, and hop and retain your balance all the time, which will enable you to defend or counter every attack instantly.

In Feng Shou there are the eighteen basic stances, which were first formulated by the Taoists some 10,000 years ago, and we shall explain these to you one by one so that you can learn to move from one to the other and thereby get the experience of trying to move on balance all the time. Remember that each stance has a job to do, so your task is to go from stance to stance and make yourself completely familiar with them, and by practising the change from one to another, you will be able to transfer your weight quickly in all directions.

Another point that must be borne in mind is that you can be attacked from any angle, without the slightest warning, so you have to learn to turn or move completely naturally and automatically. You must also adapt to your surroundings at the same time: a crowded bar where space might be very limited is vastly different to an open field. True proficiency can only come with experience, and the latter only comes through constant practise.

You will notice that nearly all the stances have the names of animals. Our ancient Chinese masters noted the particular way an animal stands and reacts and even the little habits that they adopt, and gave the name of that animal to the stance which reminded them of these various traits.

Remember that the names and the stances that are given in this book, are those used in Feng Shou, and other styles might use entirely different names for the same posture. Try to memorize the various animal names: this will save you referring back to this chapter whenever these stances are mentioned in the book.

Eagle Stance (Laoying Shih)
Stand with both feet together, and the body upright, always looking directly ahead, and the hands hanging loosely by the sides of the thighs.

Bear Stance (Hsiung Shih)

Move one foot sideways till it is about the width of your shoulders apart from the other one. Knees should be very slightly bent, and the posture upright but relaxed.

Snake Stance (She Shih)
Take one pace forward and balance your weight evenly on both legs with both knees slightly bent. This is an entirely neutral stance, enabling you to move in all directions whether defending or attacking.

Dragon Stance (Lung Shih)

From the Snake Stance move your front foot another half a pace forward, placing the majority of your body weight onto the front leg, leaning forward slightly. The back should be straight and so should the rear leg, which must be firmly planted on the floor, to reinforce the power of the hand.

Cat Stance (Mao Shih)

Bring your body weight straight back onto the rear leg, bending both knees. Now raise the heel of the front leg so that only the toes of that foot are in contact with the floor. Ensure that your balance is good on the back leg for defence and attack purposes.

Crane Stance (Hao Shih)

From the Cat Stance simply raise your front leg into the air so that it clears the ground and your front thigh is roughly parallel to the floor. The support leg should be slightly bent.

Tiger Stance (Laohu Shih)

From the Eagle or Bear Stance all you have to do for this simple posture is to throw your head sideways, and if necessary, tilt the shoulders slightly. Don't forget to practise these movements to the left and to the right to obtain maximum flexibility.

Lion Stance (Shihtzu Shih)

With your feet about the width of your shoulders apart and the knees slightly bent, turn the upper part of the body completely sideways. Throw your weight onto one leg. Concentrate on the whip-turn of the shoulders, pivoting mainly on the axis of the hips.

Leopard Stance (Pao Shih)
From Eagle or Bear Stances move one leg half a pace to one side, bending the knee of that leg and transferring most of the body weight on to it. The other leg should be kept straight and firmly planted on the floor. The body can be bent inward so that a hollow is created.

Monkey Stance (Hou Shih)
From the Dragon or Snake Stance all you need to do is bring your body weight back and place it over the rear leg, bending the knee slightly. The front leg now slides back along the floor with the foot remaining flat on the floor all the time.

Riding Horse Stance (Ch'i Ma Shih)

From the Eagle or Bear Stances, step off half a pace directly sideways, and bend both knees deeply sinking your weight downwards, and balance your body evenly on both legs. You should ensure that the body is kept erect, and that the feet are firmly planted on the floor.

Frog Stance (Wa Shih)

From the Bear Stance simply drop all your weight down to the floor, so that your bottom nearly touches it, and ensure that you maintain your balance by lightly resting your arms on or by the side of your knees.

Scissor Stance (Chientao Shih)
From the Eagle or Bear Stances place your weight onto one leg whilst the other leg is now moved beyond and behind the supporting leg, with the toes making contact with the floor. The front leg supports the majority of your body weight, and both knees should be kept bent.

Cross Leg Stance (P'anche T'ui Shih)
From the Eagle or Bear Stance put the weight of your body onto one leg, with the knee slightly bent. Now raise the other leg and place it across the front of the leg that is supporting your weight, and place the toes of the front foot gently on the floor. The weight of the body must be kept on the rear leg throughout.

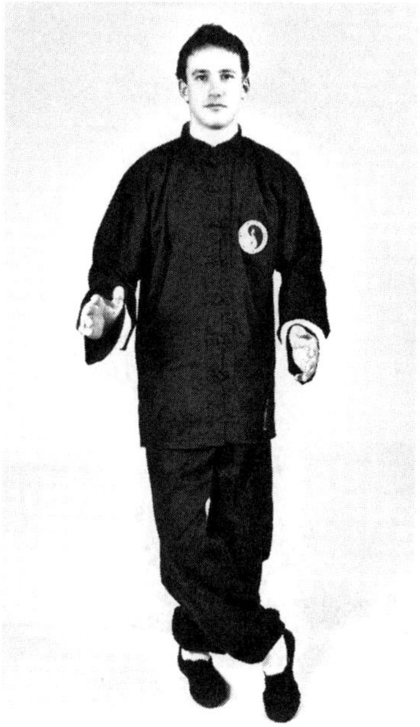

Chicken Stance (Chi Shih)

From the Eagle or Bear Stance turn the whole body sideways, take one pace forward, and as you do so bend the rear knee as deeply as possible, but keep your body upright and with perfect balance. The front foot should be flat on the floor, whilst the rear foot should be resting on the toes.

Dog Stance (Kou Shih)

From the Crane Stance just swing your front leg forward, just as if you were executing a kicking action. All your weight is maintained on your rear leg, and make sure that you keep your body upright. The front leg should be kept straight, but slightly bend the rear knee.

Horse Stance (Ma Shih)

From Eagle or Bear Stance bend the knee of one leg slightly and place your body weight on to that leg. The other leg should be taken directly out sideways on a level with your hip, whilst you allow your body to lean in the opposite direction, making sure that balance is good.

Stork Stance (Tsien Hao Shih)

Transfer your body weight onto one leg, with the body upright. Bend the knee of the other leg, and let the foot swing upwards to the rear, and at the same time point the toes. The shin of the raised leg should be approximately parallel with the floor.

Hawk Stance (Ying Shih)

From the Stork Stance simply straighten the leg that is in the air, and take it directly backwards, with the heel leading. Try to keep the knee locked, and raise it to the level of your hips. The body can be bent slightly forward to counterbalance the weight of the leg.

Drunkard Stance (Tsui Han Shih)

This is probably the most simple of all the stances, because all you have to do is to lie on your back on the floor. It is a very good idea if you learn to roll to the right and to the left, so that if you are ever attacked when you are on the ground, you can move quickly either way. Whilst on your back you can raise your knee, and bend the elbow of the arm on the same side so that it touches that knee, and you now have what we call a knee and elbow defence.

These are the first twenty stances of Feng Shou. Now endeavour to practise them constantly - not necessarily in the order that they have been presented to you - and learn to move in all directions from all the stances, until you get a smooth and continual flow of movement. Having attained this, then the next step is to slowly speed up your footwork, until you can move into and out of the postures really fast. Bear in mind that there are many more advanced stances to come, so ensure that you create a really strong foundation by practising these first basic twenty, then you will find that the others will come quite easily.

All clubs in the International Wu Shu Association throughout the world make a point of running through these stances at the beginning of every training session because it has always been an important aspect of our kung fu system. We cannot stress strongly enough the significance of this training in the long run.

It is an excellent training media to learn not only by moving from one stance to another, but also by shifting the balance quickly, by moving your weight from one leg to the other, and learning to hold it there for a minute or two, just on one leg. You can also move the leg constantly in the air from crane to hawk, then sideways into horse, then back to crane, but ensuring that at all times you maintain a good balance.

This might seem tedious and even monotonous at times, and your muscles will probably object at first, but if you are truly dedicated you will find that this practise will yield good results, such as achieving beautiful stability, controlled weight distribution, and very high speeds.

Chapter 7

Foot Flow Patterns

As the previous chapter confirms, the stance is the necessary starting point of Feng Shou movement, and perhaps the obvious progression from the movement of the feet on the ground is the movement of the feet in the air, which will increase the striking and defensive systems of anyone. But remember that the moment you lift one foot off the floor, you drastically reduce your stability and your mobility.

So there is always the danger of leaving yourself more vulnerable, especially for the inexperienced, even though you are increasing your striking power, and this is the perfect understanding of the Yin and Yang. Always bear in mind that you should never use a kicking action unless you are absolutely confident that it will be successful.

After all, if you are up against a much stronger opponent, he may only have to land one blow to end the fight, so an unwise kicking action might give him the opportunity he wants, simply because you were in no position to evade or move out of the way quickly. You already know that physical strength is not necessary, but it still does not mean that you can survive an accurately aimed blow. As a matter of fact, our aim is never to be hit, which means that at all times you have got to stay one jump ahead of your opponent. You are not exactly in this ideal situation when you are caught with one leg in the air because of an ill-timed kick. The moral is: keep both feet on the ground unless you are absolutely sure that you can lift one of them, strike, and get back into another stance before your opponent has time to retaliate.

If you are in any doubt, don't take the risk. Instead try if possible to use a hand strike, followed by whatever stance puts you in the best position to either strike again, or to defend yourself against your opponent's next move. There are many instances when you can pave the way for the kick without exposing yourself to any danger. Naturally this will come with your experience in all sections of our art, and that is why constant practise is essential. No other Chinese art in the world has the foot flow patterns that are a part of the daily training of the art of Feng Shou, but why are they so unique? Firstly, the techniques of kicking were part of the sequences handed down through the Lee family and passed to us by our most respected master Chan Kam Lee. Secondly, the foot flow patterns attached to each of the Lee family's kicking techniques were devised by myself, and I have given the copyright of these to the Association for their safe-keeping. These are the real reasons why no other style has these foot patterns or anything with the remotest resemblance to them.

They form a basic foundation for the very smooth and fast footwork of our art that enables everyone, young and old, male or female, not only to be able to kick properly and very scientifically, but also to use the feet to evade attacks, as well as learning to control the legs and the feet of your opponent, through a soft and effortless movement. It enables the muscles and the sinews of the legs to become very relaxed and supple, and yet they have the tendency to strengthen the ankles and knees so that foot evasions become exceedingly pliable.

These foot patterns are an integral part of the training of Feng Shou, but there is a lot of learning and practice that lies ahead, for there are 131 of these sequences and to be proficient in each one takes a long time and a lot of hard training. They give every student of the arts the opportunity of building up their kicking techniques, and an enormous variety of approach footwork, which includes half turns, full spins, jumping into the air, walking the air. They will aid the speedy manoeuvrability of each person, and they do all this whilst exercising their kicks either as a part of an attack movement or when utilizing the same techniques during an evasive action.

So treat these leg rhythms and foot patterns with great respect, but use them wisely, initially as a form of exercise, and don't forget to practice them only within your own personal capabilities and limitations. When it starts to become really hard work, and your muscles start to flag, then it is time to stop, and practise again another day.

Foot Pattern No. 1

Start in the right Snake posture (No. 1.1). Now move your left foot forward so that it crosses in front of your right foot, and as the left foot touches the floor turn the toes towards the left (No. 1.2). Now swing your right foot forward and upward so that it will reach your opponent's chest or even the face (No. 1.3).

As it swings down let it cross in front of your left leg, dropping on the floor beyond the left side of your own left foot (No. 1.4). Now step back one pace with your left leg and let your right foot slide back quite naturally, so that you are once again back in your right Snake stance (No. 1.5).

Now this time your partner swings his right foot into the air at you, in the same sequence of movements that you have just performed, but, as that leg floats up towards you, move your left leg back, followed by the right foot so that you are automatically moving back out of the range of his foot. He, of course, executes the same evasion movement when you swing your leg up at him. After having tried this pattern a few times in the right style, repeat it on the other leg by moving into left stance - that is, start in left snake stance and kick with your left foot.

Foot Pattern No. 1.1

Foot Pattern No. 1.2

Foot Pattern No. 1.3

Foot Pattern No. 1.4

Foot Pattern No. 1.5

Foot Pattern No. 2

Stand in right Snake stance (No. 2.1). Take a pace forward with your left foot, so that it crosses and is in front of your right foot, and turn your left foot to the left (No. 2.2). Now take a half pace forward with your right foot, turning the toes outwards to your right (No. 2.3), then swing your left foot forward and upward into the air, keeping the leg straight (No. 2.4).

Let your left leg swing back downwards, and place it on the floor after it has crossed in front of your right leg (No. 2.5), and turn the whole body quite naturally with the movement of the leg, so that your shoulders are now facing to the right. Take a pace back with your right foot, then a shorter pace with the left foot, so that you are now back in left Snake stance (No. 2.6).

As you come back, after having completed the kick, your partner comes in to you and executes the same foot flow pattern and kick, so you may have to take an extra couple of paces back in order to keep out of his range. As your partner retreats after his kick, you move in again and execute the same foot pattern, but this time from the left stance which you are now in from your first kick attempt. So from your left Snake stance, you step off and cross with your right foot, take a half pace with the left leg, kick with your right foot, swing down in front of your left leg, then step back with the left foot allowing the right foot to slice back slightly, and you are once more back in right Snake stance. Then your partner does the same, and so on, until you have repeated the sequence a few times each.

Foot Pattern No. 2.1

Foot Pattern No. 2.2

Foot Pattern No. 2.3

Foot Pattern No. 2.4

Foot Pattern No. 2.5

Foot Pattern No. 2.6

Foot Pattern No. 3

This is a simple combination of foot patterns Nos. 1 and 2. Again start off in the right Snake stance (not shown). Take a pace forward with your left foot and the toes turning out (No. 3.1), then as soon as that foot touches the floor, swing the right foot up into the air (No. 3.2), just as you did in Pattern No. 1. Now, as your right foot comes down, place it on the floor about a half pace ahead of the left foot, with your right toes pointing out, then immediately swing your left foot straight up into the air (No. 3.3). You will notice that this gives you a double kicking action, with both legs swinging up into the air. As your left foot drops down let it cross in front of and beyond your right leg (No. 3.4), and turn your body towards the right as well, just as you did in Pattern No. 2. Now take a pace with your right foot, and allow the left foot to slide back half a pace, and you now finish in left Snake stance (No. 3.5).

Again, as in Pattern No. 2, as you retreat your partner moves in to execute the same kick pattern as yourself, and you retreat from his advancing attack. As soon as he has finished his kicks, you move forward again to execute the same kick pattern, and he in turn retreats away from your attack. Remember that you are now in a left Snake stance, and so both of you are alternating your stances, as you practise the flowing movements in and out of this particular foot flow pattern. Repeat them a few times each until you get the feel of it.

Foot Pattern No. 3.1

Foot Pattern No. 3.2

Foot Pattern No. 3.3

Foot Pattern No. 3.4

Foot Pattern No. 3.5

Foot Pattern No. 4

Stand in right Snake stance. Take a half pace forward with your right foot, with the toes pointing out towards the right. Bring your left foot forward, then spin your foot and your body round in almost a full clockwise circle, pivoting on the whole of your right foot - don't pivot on just the ball of the foot or you will have a tendency to weaken your 'roots'. Put your left foot down onto the floor in front of your right foot, and, at this point you should be facing towards what was your left side and your body should be facing the same direction as your left foot. Now draw your right knee up into the air, so that your right foot is near to your bottom, then shoot your leg out sideways in a side kicking action, making sure that you lock your right knee when the leg is fully straight. Let your right leg now swing down towards the floor, first crossing in front of your left leg, then taking it just beyond your left foot. As soon as your right foot touches the floor, place your weight upon it, so that you can take a pace back with the left foot. Then allow the right foot to slide back about a half a pace, and you should now be back in right Snake stance.

Foot Pattern No. 4

Towards the end of your kicking technique, as you begin to retreat, your partner moves towards you to execute the same foot pattern. Do this a few times from the right stance, then swap over and try it from the left stance. That is, start in left Snake stance, take a half pace forward with your left foot, a full spin with the right foot, then kick sideways with the left foot and leg. Replace your left foot on the floor beyond your right foot, then take a pace back with the right foot, slide the left foot back slightly and you should now be in left Snake stance once again.

When you first execute Foot Pattern No. 4, try to keep your leg parallel with the floor during the kicking action, and later on you will be able to slowly raise the height of the foot, as your muscles become more flexible. Another important point is that you must learn to kick with the heel of the foot, and not with the toes, and this will give you a much better muscle change in the leg, so ensure that you pull your toes back and let the heel lead the foot.

From now on, every fourth foot pattern is a new technique, i.e. Nos. 4, 8,12,16 and so on, whereas the intermediate numbers are combinations of each of the fourth pattern coupled with either foot pattern Nos. 1, 2 or 3. For instance:

Foot Pattern No. 5

This is a combination of Pattern No. 1 and Pattern No. 4 executed in that order. (1 and 4 adds up to 5.) In other words, you first perform Foot Pattern No. 1, then once you have replaced your right foot down onto the floor, which you do as if you were going to take a pace forward, then you spin-step on the left foot and execute Pattern No. 4. When your partner executes the same pattern, you will have to move back at least two paces because of the distance that you have covered when you advance to execute this combination of foot patterns.

Foot Pattern No. 6

This harmonizes Pattern No. 2 with Pattern No. 4. (2 and 4 adds up to 6.) Go through the motions of executing Foot Pattern No. 2, but, as the foot swings down, place it on the floor about one pace ahead of your other foot, now spin-step, and then move into Pattern No. 4. Remember that Foot Pattern No. 2 alters your finishing stance: for instance, if you start in right stance you should finish in left stance, and vice versa, so you will find that this pattern will alter the finishing stance of any combination technique that is harmonized with it.

Foot Pattern No. 7

The amalgamation of Pattern No. 3 with Pattern No. 4 makes Pattern No. 7, and this is executed in a similar fashion to Pattern No. 6, by spin-stepping on the right foot before following on with Pattern No. 4. You will, no doubt, have realized that the foot flow patterns are now really becoming interesting, but the work load is also increasing and that means you will have to get more regular practice if your skill is to make steady improvement in the future.

Foot Pattern No. 8

This is very similar to Pattern No. 4, but in this case there are no spin-steps. Start off in right Snake posture, now take a pace forward with your right foot, then bring the left foot forward until it is alongside your right foot, and then place the weight of your body fully onto your left leg. Now draw your right knee up, and shoot the right leg out sideways in a side kick (Horse stance), locking the right knee, and keeping the leg parallel to the floor. Replace your right foot onto the floor but first cross it in front of the left leg. Take a pace to the rear with the left foot, followed by a shorter pace with the right foot, and you are once again back in your right stance. As you retreat, after having put your right foot down onto the floor, so your partner advances and executes the same kicking action from his right stance too. Try this a few times to get the 'feel' of the rhythm, then both you and your partner change over to the left stance, and try it by taking the pace forward with the left foot, bringing the right foot up to the side of the left foot, then transferring your body weight onto your right leg, then draw the left knee up and continue its flow of movement by kicking directly out sideways. Don't forget to lock the left knee as you straighten your leg. Let the left leg swing down after the kick, cross it in front of the right leg, and place it on the floor. Step back in retreat with the right foot which is immediately followed by the left, and you should now be in left Snake stance.

Foot Pattern No. 9

This starts off with Foot Pattern No. 1 and then it is combined with Foot Pattern No. 8 which immediately follows on in a continuous flow of movement. In other words, it is similar to Foot Pattern No. 5, but in this instance there is no spin-step.

Foot Pattern No. 10

This is a combination of Foot Pattern No. 2 which is immediately followed by Foot Pattern No. 8. You know how Pattern No. 2 changes the style that you finish in, so remember you will be completing these two combined techniques in left stance if you have started from a right style posture.

Foot Pattern No. 11

Foot Pattern No. 3 commences this particular foot flow pattern and it is immediately followed by Foot Pattern No. 8. At this stage you should find that all these kick techniques are becoming much easier to perform, and now it is beginning to be fun to practise, especially as your muscles should now be more relaxed and flexible. You should be moving more fluently and faster, but don't let speed make you get careless in the execution of a perfect technique. Speed is the very last hurdle that you ought to think about, if you intend to be not only good, but outstanding in these arts. Slowness breeds perfection, for in China we understand that all things are born of Yin within nature, and slowness is Yin.

Foot Pattern No. 12

Start off in right Snake stance. Take a half pace forward with the right foot, toes pointing to the right as it comes to rest on the floor. Bring your left foot forward, and spin your leg and body round in an almost full clockwise circle, with the body weight moving onto the left leg as soon as it touches the floor. Now swing your right foot from left to right also in a clockwise direction, but using the back heel of your right foot in a back scooping action. Your foot should be parallel to the floor to start with, and you can increase or decrease the height of it, as you gain more dexterity and experience.

Replace your right foot back onto the floor, by allowing it to swing behind your left leg, and just beyond the heel of your left foot. Take your left foot backwards one pace, by transferring your weight onto your right leg, for you are now about to retire, and then you allow the right foot to slide back also, by placing your weight onto your left leg as soon as it rests on the floor. You should now be back in your right Snake stance.

On your retreating movement, your partner should be coming towards you, to execute the same kick pattern. Try the flow continuously, backwards and forwards, between your partner and yourself for a number of times. Then switch over into left Snake stance, and try it with your left foot as well. That is, take a half pace forward with the left foot, spin-step on your right leg, back heel with your left foot, and cross your left foot behind your right foot before putting it on the ground. As soon as the left foot rests on the floor put your body weight on to it, so that you can now step back one pace with your right foot. Now put your weight on to your right leg, and allow the left foot to slide back a short distance. You are now back into left Snake stance.

With all these kicking patterns, once you have attained a general idea of them, then you can vary the height of the kicks as it pleases you, and by so doing you can enlarge the scope of your skill.

Remember to always practise slowly until you have attained the smooth flow of a particular technique, and are able to do it without having to think where the feet must go, which leg should be supporting your body weight, which directions your toes should be pointing, and which way your shoulders should be turning or leaning. Once you can do all these things without having to stop to think, then, and only then, should you consider building up your speeds.

Once you have attained absolute perfection in the execution of the techniques, and have built up your speeds, then the final stage is to learn to jump into the air, or what we call 'flighting' the kick, by taking off on the leg that is supporting your weight. Foot Flow Pattern No. 3 is probably the easiest one to flight at first, and Pattern No. 1 you may find quite a tough one to do. You have the rest of your life to gain this sort of experience, so don't be in too great a hurry. Time may seem short at times, but it is actually infinite, so don't try and rush yourself.

Chapter 8

Striking Units

You can handle any situation of attack in either of two ways. The first way is to have a go with complete disregard for the safety of your own body, by mastering all your brute strength, and together with a huge piece of luck you might be able to get out of the particular situation fairly lightly, maybe with only a couple of black eyes, perhaps a broken nose, or just a few cuts and bruises. If you happen to be stronger and taller than your opponent, then there are always the long odds that you could win, even though you might end up a bit battle scarred.

The second, alternative way is to defend yourself intelligently, which is what this book is all about. Always remember that Feng Shou kung fu is not a power struggle, so you do not have to meet your assailant in a head-on collision. By using your skill carefully, you can patiently wait for the moment when your attacker shows up his many weaknesses, using your feet and knowledge to keep you just out of trouble all the time. When your moment does come, you will be able to get through his defences in a split second, strike as many times as you wish, and get out again without giving him the slightest chance of countering your movement.

This is where your training and practice come in, moving the feet to help evade all the attacks, dodging all the blows or warding them off whether they are a long or short range attack, mentally alert to watch and note his points of strength or his weakness (the latter being the most important). You do not have to treat it as a boxing match where you stand and swap punches, for that would severely limit your potential, your capabilities, as well as your technique and skill.

Your hands can be used not only as a means of self-defence but as an infinite variety of uses and it is a shame to hamper their versatility by just holding them into fists as most western people do. In China the closed fist is regarded as a very weak and a very vulnerable unit of the hand. If you hit someone hard on the chin you might knock him out, but you could also break some bones in your hand or cause yourself unnecessary damage. If there is more than one attacker, and you have put one or even both hands out of action due to injury, then you have severely hampered your chances of ultimate survival.

In contrast, the open hand is very much stronger, less prone to injury, has greater flexibility, and can change from one type of striking unit to another very quickly. It has a larger variety of angles for use in counter-attacks, and when it is combined with the Ch'i, then its potential force is really dynamic.

Perhaps the greatest example of the versatility of the open hand in Feng Shou is the 'invisible' striking techniques. This may seem too difficult to believe, but you can stand directly in front of your opponent, and strike a blow at him which he will never see, but will certainly feel. This might sound an impossibility but it is true, as all the high grade students of our Association will tell you.

However, whether we strike with the open hand or the clenched fist, we use both to their fullest advantage; in fact, we have the greatest variety of strikes and punches out of all the boxing styles in the world.

These styles include strikes which are long, short, straight, curled, hooked, forwards, sideways, up and down, and backwards. In addition, our hand formations consist of the open hand, clenched fist, side fists, back fists, round fists, curled hand, hooked hand, one finger, two fingers, hooked fingers, side hand, claw hand, back hand, and many more besides. Although we shall be describing only fifteen of them in this chapter, there are more to come which will be included in further books.

Each striking unit has a specific job to do, and this is determined by the range, angle, position, stance and particular target to be aimed at. You must learn to use each one and manipulate your hands, fingers, knuckles and wrist quickly so that you can change from one to another in a split second.

Read the instructions carefully, and practise them over and over again, checking each time that your positioning conforms to the instructions and the illustrations that follow.

Open Hand (Chang Shou)
Pull your fingers back by flexing the wrist, and make sure that the fingers are kept straight all the time, although they don't necessarily have to be kept together. The strike should be made with the heel of the palm.

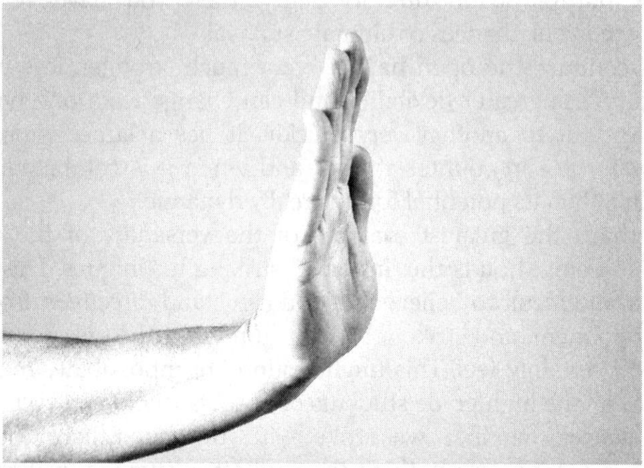

Poisoned Hand (Tu Shou)
This is another open hand technique, but keep the tips of the fingers pulled in by bending the first two knuckles of your fingers, and strike with the heel of the palm. Keep the thumb close to the side of the palm.

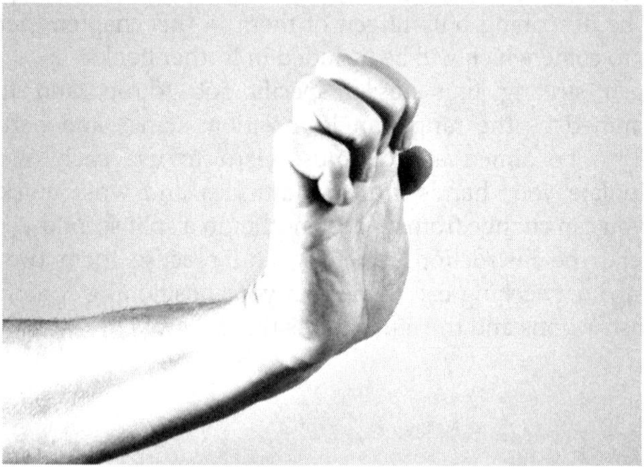

Hand Sword (Shou Tao)

Open the hand by stiffening the fingers, ensuring that they are all kept close together, including the thumb which should also be held close to the side of the palm. The strike is made with the little finger edge of the palm. The best area to strike with is approximately one inch (25mm) below the base of the little finger to about one inch below the base of the palm.

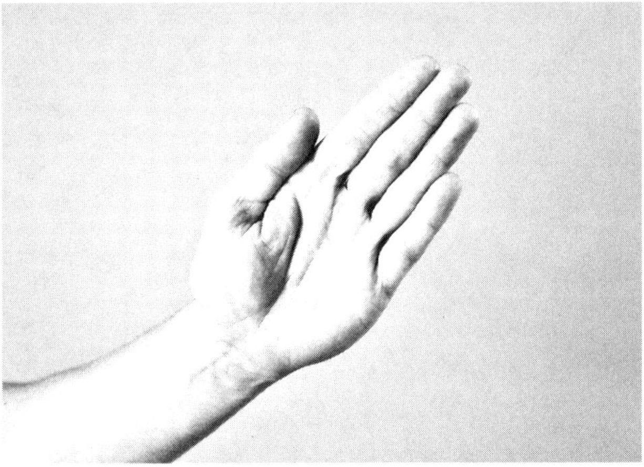

Straight Fist (Ch'uan T'ou)

This means closing the hand into a very tight ball, striking with the knuckles of the hand, whilst making sure that the arm is kept straight. The best area of the fist to strike with, when using the straight fist, is the first two large knuckles.

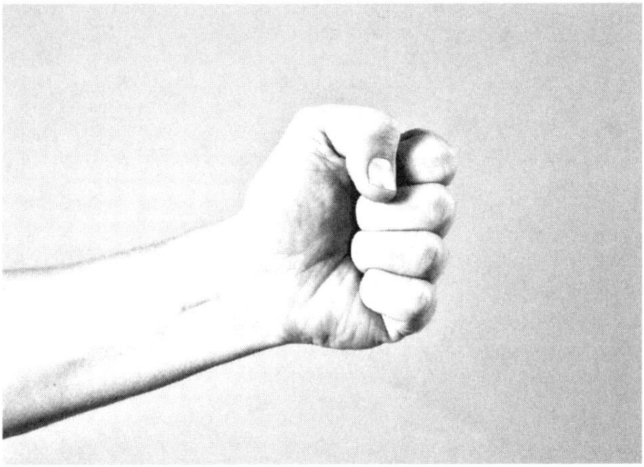

Eagle Claw (Laoying Chao)

The fingers of the open hand are slightly bent and stiffened and represent the talons of the eagle's foot. These talons are normally used for scratching, gouging, and especially for gripping.

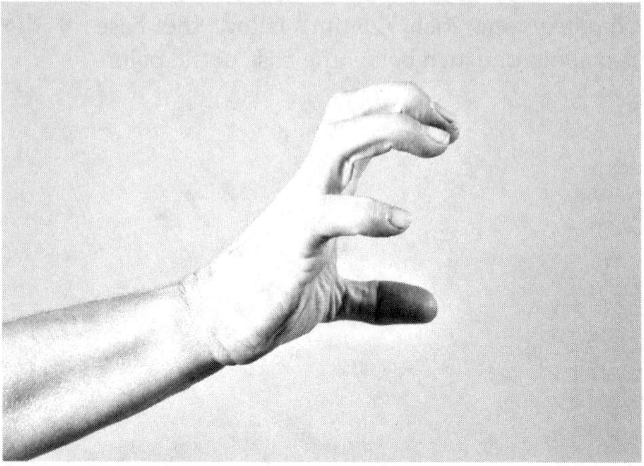

Crab Claw (Hsiech'ien)

This is the use of the thumb and the first finger of either hand, and bowed so that a grip can be made, if required, on various parts of your opponent's body such as the wrist or the back of the neck.

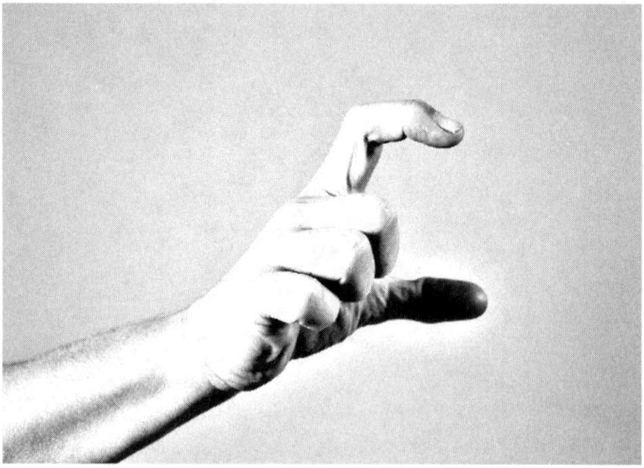

One Finger Spear (I Chih Ch'iang)
The first finger is stretched out straight, whilst all the other fingers are kept bent, to keep the way clear for the jab of the one finger.

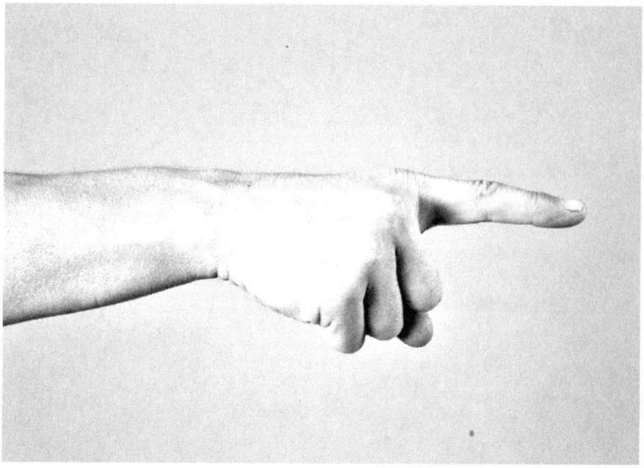

Two Finger Spear (Liang Chih Ch'iang)
Separate the first two fingers of the hand, whilst keeping all the other fingers bent. This type of spear is usually utilized against the eyes, so the fingers need to be apart to span the bridge of the nose.

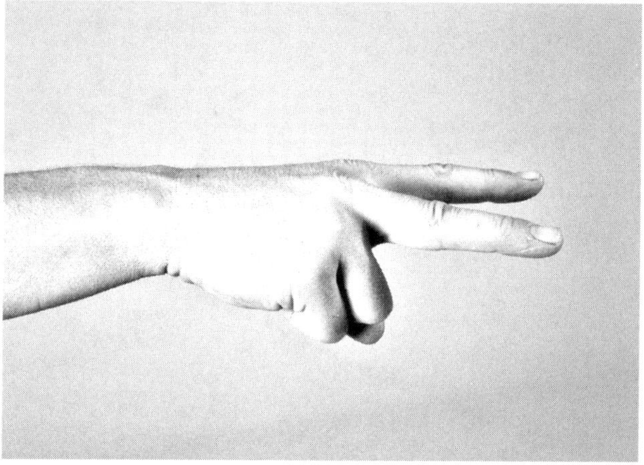

Eye of the Phoenix (Fenghuang Yenching)
Clench the fist, but let the index finger protrude, so that it looks like a tight hook, now give it support from underneath with the thumb. The strike is made on the knuckle of the first finger.

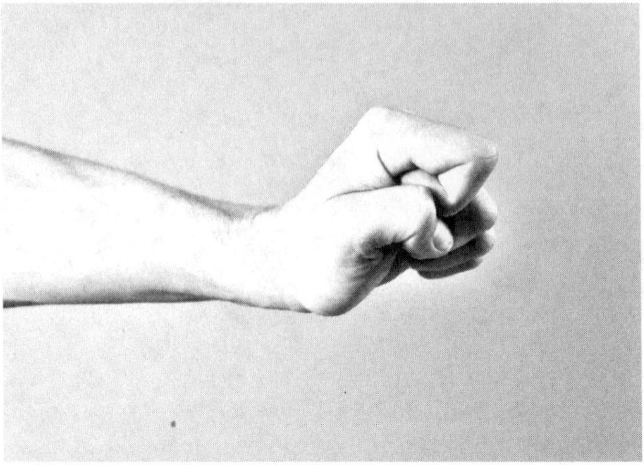

Hammer Fist (Ch'uan Ch'ui)
This is also a closed fist, but instead of using the front knuckles to strike with, the strike is made from a side-on position so that contact is made on the little finger edge of the palm.

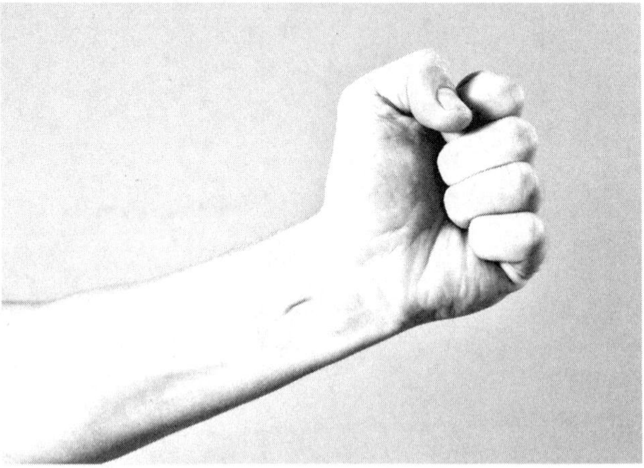

Minor Hammer Fist (Hsiao Ch'ui Ch'uant ou)
A closed fist with the thumb tucked inside the first finger, and you actually strike with the back of the thumb.

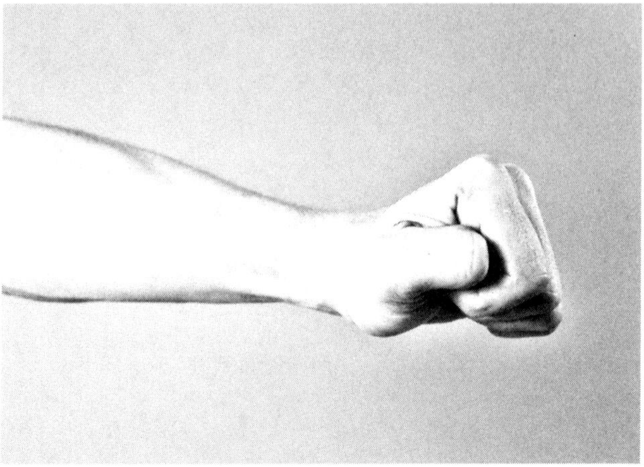

Leopard Fist (Pao Ch'uan)
Clench the fingers so that they all bend at the second knuckle. The strike is made on the points of these knuckles, with the main force spread over the first three.

Tiger's Head (Laohu T'ou)
Clench the fingers but allow the second finger to protrude in a hook and then be reinforced by the thumb underneath. The strike is made with the tip of the second knuckle of that finger.

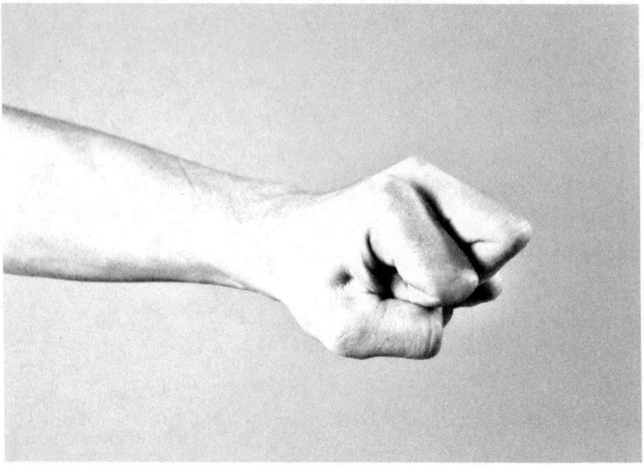

Elbow Spear (Kepochou Ch'iang)
This simply makes use of the elbow to strike with, but not only do we utilize the point of the elbow, but we also use the underside and the back of the elbow.

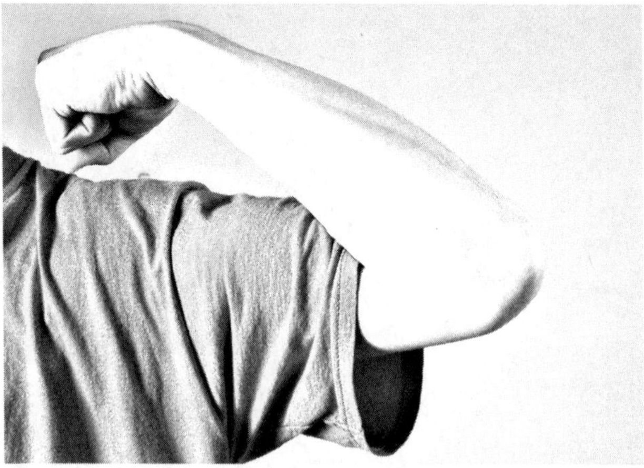

Hand Spear (Shou Ch'iang)
This is the open hand with the fingers strongly extended, and the strike is made by thrusting with the fingertips.

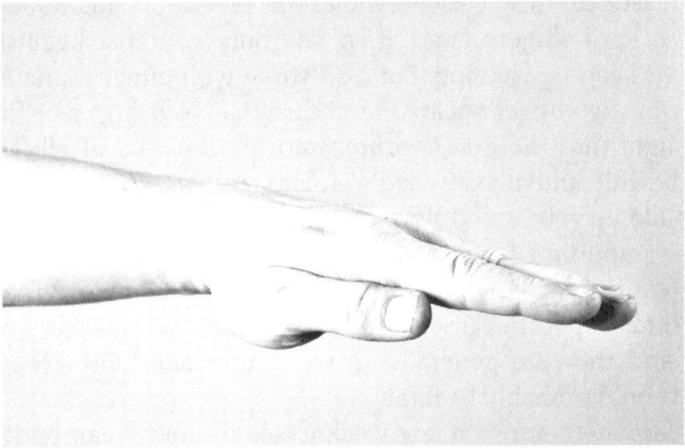

Not only are there many other striking units, but there is also the huge range of techniques that come from the correct utilization of the feet, knees, shoulders, hips and head. For the moment, however, simply remember that it is not the vastness of your acquired knowledge that will save your life, but your skill and the experience with the small amount of technique that you have at your finger tips. In other words, get down to the task of practising constantly, so that you can slowly build up the range of your skill, and you will be able to look after yourself in a crisis, when your life might depend upon it.

There are certain aids which will help you with your striking practice, so that not only will you build up the power of the arm when executing any of the blows, but you will develop great accuracy when striking.

Hang a lightweight sheet of cardboard, which should be about six inches (15cm) square, from two corners in an open doorway. The idea is to strike at the cardboard, but at no time should you actually touch it. If you stop just short of the target, the air current in front of the hand should make it start to swing. The object is to keep the cardboard swinging without actually touching it at any time during practice. If you should happen to touch the cardboard at any time, stop the card from swinging, and start your striking practice again. Once you can do this with the open hand and can keep it swinging continuously without touching it, then the next stage is to clench your hand into a fist, and strike at the same target with the knuckles of the fist. Again make sure that you do not touch the cardboard at any time, and keep it swinging continuously by the pressure of air in front of your fist. After you have mastered this, cut two holes in the cardboard about the width of two fingers apart. Use not only your fist against the target to keep it swinging, but also strike with either a one finger spear or a two finger spear, and ensure that your finger or fingers go straight into the holes without moving the card at all. This is very difficult and needs deadly accuracy. Practise slowly at first then build up your speed slowly.

It is important to get used to the fact that you should never make contact with the cardboard, because the points that we concentrate upon in our style of kung fu are the soft parts of the body, and they are generally so weak that one blow accurately placed could probably be fatal.

In fact there are so many weaknesses in the human body that practice of the art should be carried out with extreme caution. Never, under any circumstances, should you deliberately strike your opponent in practice, for even the weight of your little finger on his chest bone, if there was a slight weakness there, could cause a hair-line fracture, or worse if he should happen to have brittle bones.

Our art can be so devastating that it demands you to be constantly at one with yourself, with complete self-control and self-discipline at all times. This is particularly true if you happen to meet a crisis when you have little or no time to think, and so you must rely completely on your reflex action, your experience and your training.

Chapter 9

Ward-Offs

The hands can be lethal weapons if you know how to use them properly, and the body can be very vulnerable, if you know where to strike and what type of hand weapon to use at that specific point. In fact you only need to get one blow through your opponent's defence, landing it on your chosen target, and it could well be the end of the contest. However, if your opponent should happen to get his blow in first, it could well put the end to the bout and to you as well.

So, the first rule is to ensure that you don't get hit at any time, no matter what the angle of the strike might be, even by a sudden or unexpected attack. This is extremely important, and we can never stress this enough — more important in fact than anything else that you might learn in Feng Shou, and it should take priority over any other series of techniques.

Remember also that Feng Shou is primarily an art of self-defence, and as such you should never be the one that strikes the first blow. In fact, you should never strike a blow at all unless it is absolutely unavoidable, or it is the very last resort after all other means for a peaceful settlement have failed.

Nevertheless, this does not mean that you have to lose face. On the contrary, in a street fight it is much more impressive as well as very effective to glide past all of your antagonist's attacks. Of course, while you are doing this you can make it very apparent that you could have easily hit him if you had so wished. By the time you have fully mastered the techniques in this book you will have the confidence and the ability to out-manoeuvre anyone, unless you happen to meet one of our more experienced Feng Shou students and masters.

You cannot hide this kind of self-confidence, and you will find that it is a very effective deterrent to any would-be attacker;

invariably trouble will pass you by without having to resort to the use of the arts.

You already know the stances, and by practising them you will have seen how moving from one stance to another takes various parts of your body out of reach, and therefore out of range of your opponent's blows. If you utilize the stances alone, they would certainly enable you to avoid almost all attacks, and that is without using your own hands and arms in self-protection.

But if you bring your hands and arms into play — formidable as you would be through your stances alone — your abilities will increase beyond all recognition.

In the gentle and soft art of Feng Shou, we have three basic ways of defending ourselves against an opponent's blows. The first is called a 'block' (Tang) and it merely involves stopping an opponent's blow or kick, with either an arm or hand, in mid-air. Boxers use this mode of stopping a blow quite a lot, so no doubt you are familiar with it, and appreciate what we mean. However, we use this very seldom in our art because the process of blocking means relying on brute physical strength, which also means that you have to oppose force. That is something we always try to avoid since it is against the principles of the soft arts of China. It is far better to use the second way, known as 'parry' (Pien-i), which is a light brushing action of the hand, wrist or arm to divert the blow. In some cases all that is needed is a gentle turn of the wrist to parry even the strongest punch. Many people, particularly in the West, use far more force than is necessary to defend themselves, and thereby burn up their energies needlessly. The art of Feng Shou is such a sensitive art that everything should be executed in the same relaxed, soft, rhythmic style, using only the minimum amount of force at all times.

Our third defensive technique is the 'ward-off' (Tangkai), which is very similar to the parry except that it involves a much longer action towards the end of the technique, to take an opponent's strike well clear of its target. The parry is often just a twist of the wrist, but when used effectively it is enough to throw a punch well off its intended course.

Both of the latter techniques can be used in such a way that once you have deflected the blow you can easily counter by moving your opponent's arm and body in a straight line, round the angle of your own body, downward to the floor, or even upwards to the heavens — whichever angle is suitable for you to upset his balance, and to put him under your complete control.

These are simple basic principles, and you should carefully study the series of ward-off movements. It will be easier if you can get a friend to work with you so you can both take it in turns to act as the attacker or the defender.

Of course, there may be times that you wish to practice quietly on your own, and the best way to do this is to try all the movements in front of a mirror. Throw the punch at your reflection in the mirror, make a mental note of the angle and the path that the blow took, then practise the appropriate ward-off or parry that may suit it at the time.

Now, you and your partner face one another in right Snake Stance to begin with, with both hands in front of the chest, as if you were on guard. Your partner should now move into Dragon Stance (Lung Shih), and aim a straight arm blow directly at your chin. You will then parry or effect a ward-off against his blow with one of the following techniques. Remember that you should both move very slowly at first to acquire the 'feel' of the parry or the ward-off, to correct any mistakes that may arise. The hardest thing to learn is to keep very soft all the time, whilst you acquire the experience. Keeping soft and gentle will certainly be a new experience to most of you, so it may take time to begin to

understand it, and to have confidence in it. So don't rush yourself, give yourself time for the natural benefits of this wonderful art to show themselves to you. Once you have acquired them you will never look back, for you will realize that the future of your experience is only one step ahead.

Sun Palm Techniques (Chih Chang)

1. Sun Palm (Chih Chang)

As the first punch comes towards you, move your weight backwards onto your rear leg, so that you are either in Cat Stance or Monkey Stance. Place your open left hand on the outside of your opponent's arm (little finger side of his arm), and rotate your wrist so that eventually your own palm faces you, and at the same time as you gently spin your hand also softly push his arm away from your chin.

2. *Sun Palm (Chih Chang)*

As the second blow comes towards you, move back so that your body weight is once again on the rear leg. This time, place your right open hand on his arm, rotate your wrist so that your own palm is towards you, and simultaneously gently push his arm to your left, and away from your chin.

3. *Sun Palm Up (Chih Chang Tai)*

This ward-off can be executed with either the left or the right palm, which is placed directly underneath your opponent's arm. With a gentle lift and push upward you can take this arm directly upwards and over your own head. To check to see if you are doing it correctly, the palm of your hand should be flat against his arm to start with, and as you take his arm over the top of your head, his arm should be in contact with the little finger edge of your palm.

4. *Sun Palm Down (Chih Chang Hsia)*

Again either hand can be utilized to effect this ward-off, so as his blow is delivered at your chin, place your open hand on top of his arm, and press down very firmly. In this particular case, it has to be pushed down very fast.

5. *Double Sun Palm (Shuang Chih Chang)*

You may find that this is a little difficult to execute at first, because not only do you have to transfer your weight on to your rear leg, but you must also keep your body to your left. Once your wrists become supple through constant practise it will become quite easy. Just ensure that both palms push your opponent's arm away from its intended target, your chin, and past your right shoulder.

6. *Double Sun Palm (Shuang Chih Chang)*

This is exactly the same technique as the movement explained in No. 5 but, as you can see from the photograph, the ward-off is effected from the inside of your opponent's arm, and you gently push his arm and hand past your left shoulder.

7. *Double Sun Palm Up (Shuang Chih Chang Tai)*

As the next blow comes towards your chin, put the bottom of both of your palms together so that they are touching near to your wrists. Then raise both palms upward, making contact with your opponent's arm and then push his blow up and above your head.

8. *Double Sun Palm Down (Shuang Chih Chang Hsia)*
This can be executed in two different ways: you can have one hand on top of the other, or you can have both hands positioned side-by-side. Press your opponent's arm towards the floor, but make sure you press fast and very firmly.

9. *Sun Palm — Outside Left (Chih Chang — Waimien Tsuo)*
If your opponent's blow comes towards your stomach, ward-off with the palm of your left hand on the elbow side of his arm, with your fingers pointing down. Ensure that your fingers are kept together, and your hand is firm, and press strongly so that his arm is taken past your right hip.

10. Sun Palm — Outside Right — (Chih Chang — Waimien Yu)
Your opponent strikes again towards your mid-ribs, and this time you ward-off his arm on his elbow side, with your right hand, again diverting his blow past your right side. Again make sure that your fingers are pointing down towards the floor, and keep them together.

11. Sun Palm — Inside Left (Chih Chang — Limien Tsuo)
As the next blow comes towards your stomach, use your open left palm on the inside of your opponent's arm, and ward- off his strike so that his hand or fist flows past the left side of your body. Keep your fingers and thumb close together and pointing downwards.

12. Sun Palm — Inside Right (Chih Chang — Limien Yu)
As your opponent strikes again at your belt-line, make contact with his arm in exactly the same way as you did in No. 11, but this time you will use your right hand to deflect the blow past the left side of your body. Keep the fingers together and pointing downwards.

13. Double Sun Palm — Outside (Shuang Chih Chang — Waimien)
This ward-off can be effected in two ways: you can have one hand resting on top of the other, or both hands can be in position side-by-side on his arm. The photo shows both palms warding off in the second position, and the blow is being deflected past your right side.

14. Double Sun Palm — Inside (Shuang Chih Chang — Limien)

This is the same as No. 13, but this time you reverse your two palm ward-offs by making contact on the inside of your opponent's arm. Sweep his strike past the left side of your waist or past your left hip, depending on the height of his blow.

15. Sun Palm Down (Chih Chang Hsia)

This ward-off, from another low blow can be effected in two ways: use only one hand or use both hands together. The photo shows both hands being used on top of your opponent's arm. Make sure that you press down firmly and very speedily.

Cloudy Palm Techniques (Yin Chang)

16. Cloudy Palm (Yin Chang)
If your opponent aims a blow at your face just move your weight back on to your rear leg, and make contact with his arm with the back of your right hand, on the elbow side. Gently turn your head so that eventually your palm faces towards him, and, still moving gently, push away his arm so that the blow is deflected past the right side of your head.

17. Cloudy Palm (Yin Chang)
This ward-off is the same as No. 16, but this time use your left back hand, on the thumb side of your attacker's arm. Gently push and deflect his blow past the left side of your head. Keep the fingers firmly together, turning your hand until it faces your opponent.

18. Cloudy Palm — Left (Yin Chang — Tsuo)

As your opponent aims his blow at your stomach, again automatically move your weight onto your rear leg. Quickly circle your left arm over his arm and place your left back hand on the inside of his arm, diverting his blow past your left hip, and making sure that you gently but continuously push his arm away from yourself.

19. Cloudy Palm — Right (Yin Chang — Yu)

The technique is the same as No. 18, but this time swing your right arm over the top of your attacker's arm so that you make contact with the back of your right hand on the elbow side of his arm. Gently press and sweep his blow past the line of your right hip.

Sun and Cloudy Palm Techniques (Chihe Yin Chang)

20. Sun and Cloudy Palm — Outside
(Chihe Yin Chang — Waimien)
As your opponent's blow comes towards your chin, use the left hand in a Sun Palm action and the right back hand in a Cloudy Palm technique, and you have an immediate and very strong ward-off. The whole movement is a very natural one to execute.

21. Sun and Cloudy Palm — Inside
(Chihe Yin Chang — Limien)
Another blow comes directly at your face, and you ward-off the attack by making contact with the inside of your assailant's arm, but this time use your right hand in the Sun Palm technique, whilst the left back hand becomes the Cloudy Palm.

22. Sun and Cloudy Palm — Outside
(Chihe Yin Chang — Waimien)
Your opponent strikes at your stomach, and this time use No. 20 in a reverse position, making contact on the elbow side of his arm, with the fingers of both hands pointing down towards the floor, moving his blow away from its target and past your right side.

23. Sun and Cloudy Palm — Inside
(Chihe Yin Chang — Limien)
Another blow towards the waistline is easily deflected past your left hip, by simply using this double hand technique. The left back hand becomes the Cloudy Palm and the front right hand is the Sun Palm ward-off, with both hands gently easing the blow away from its intended target.

Arm Techniques (Pei)

24. Arm Ward-Off (Pei Tang Kai)

The whole arm can be used to ward-off your opponent's blow, from the elbow to the wrist. In this case you will notice that the first contact with your opponent is with the thumb edge of your right arm. Now slowly turn your arm so that your own palm rotates inwards, and you will see his arm slowly moves away and is therefore diverted from its original target.

25. Arm Ward-Off (Pei Tang Kai)

Whereas No. 24 shows the arm of your opponent being warded off on the elbow side of his arm, this one shows the ward-off being effected on the inside of his arm. The little finger edge of your arm makes initial contact then rotate the wrist to complete the deflection.

26. Arm Ward-Off — Inside (Pei Tang Kai — Limien)
In Nos. 24 and 25 both of those ward-offs have been executed through the use of the right arm, this one shows you how it can be done using the left arm. Make contact with the thumb edge of your arm, then rotate your wrist inward to get a good diversion.

27. Arm Ward-Off — Outside (Pei Tang Kai — Waimien)
Another blow towards your face, and this time ward-off with your left arm on the elbow side of your opponent's arm. After contact is made with the little finger edge of your arm, then turn the wrist so that you can see your own palm throughout the whole movement, and watch his blow go sailing harmlessly past your body.

28. Arm Ward-Off — Right (Pei Tang Kai — Yu)
Against a low blow aimed at your stomach simply circle your right arm over your attacker's arm and then easily sweep your arm to your right, making contact on the elbow side of his arm. You will see his blow go past your right hip, as you divert it.

29. Arm Ward-Off — Left (Pei Tang Kai — Tsuo)
This is similar to the arm ward-off executed in No. 28, against a strike at the abdomen, but this time utilize the effectiveness of your left arm, by circling over the top of your assailant's arm, and making contact on the inside of his arm. As soon as you touch, sweep the arm past your left hip.

Willow Tree Techniques (Liu Shu)

30. Willow Tree — Left (Liu Shu — Tsuo)
With a blow coming at your mid-rib, just let your arm hang down with your elbow pointing forward. You will see that you will ward-off your opponent's blow with the little finger edge of your arm. Now turn your body to the right with the motion of your arm, and his blow will float past your body.

31. Willow Tree — Right (Liu Shu — Yu)
This is the same action as No. 30, and performed against another blow at your stomach. This time use your right arm, ensuring that your right elbow points towards your opponent, turn your body to the left, and his arm will be swept past the left side of your body.

These are but a few of the many ward-offs, parries, and blocks in the art of Feng Shou. You should not only practise with a partner, using your right and left arms and hands continuously, but also practise your movements in front of a mirror so that you can correct your technique. Admittedly, you won't be able to get the exact feel of actual contact but at least it helps to correct the movement of the ward-off.

Don't forget to practise on both sides of the body, and learn to execute all the techniques whether you stand in a left stance or a right stance, until every ward-off becomes second nature to you. This is important for if at any time you have to defend yourself, you may only have a split second to do so, and so your own reaction and defence must come automatically. This can only happen through regular and continuous practice, day in and day out.

Eventually you will obtain an instinctive reflex, where you will apply the correct technique with split-second timing, at the appropriate moment, and it will then become a completely natural movement and extremely effective. Through constant practice over a long period of time, you will learn to 'feel' your opponent's intentions even before he strikes, but the first step to acquire this sensitivity is through the medium of hand or arm contact.

This is another important aspect of the soft arts, which gives us quite a big advantage over our opponents, and to develop this 'feel' you must practise the art of 'I Fu Shou' (Adhering Hand), which is another step to be conquered.

Chapter 10

Roll-Aways

If you have read everything so far and have practised diligently, you will be building up a sufficient stock of information and experience to enable you to cope with the majority of situations that may arise. In any combat situation it is impossible to predict what will happen until seconds beforehand. Thus, to ensure that you are fully equipped, you need to know what to do, how to do it, and what the results of your actions will be. The correct reactions must be natural and completely instinctive, and this comes only through constant practise.

So, all that remains for you now is to get in as much practice as possible, both in a strictly controlled situation, where you are dealing with pre-arranged or specific moves or trying to improve your technique, reaction, and split-second timing in a situation which has not been preset. This latter situation is the sort of practice session where you and your partner do not stick to a set routine, and you have not arranged beforehand what you intend to do. You can resort to the many variations of ward-offs that you have learnt so far, and put them into practice when the opportunity occurs, or when you feel that you should try a certain move or deviation.

By doing so, often enough, you will find that every situation covered in this book will come up from time to time, so you will be able to practise every way of attack, defence, and counter attack that you have learnt so far. Eventually the right reactions to any given situation or mode of attack will become second nature to you.

The finest foundation for this spontaneous movement comes in our 'roll-away' (Chuan Shen) system. It is a progression of continuous movements, which involves attack, defence, and counter attack, by both you and your partner, and it is executed in a non-stop, constant flowing motion. No other kung fu system in the world incorporates this unique system of training, for it was devised by myself from the basis of the Three Star Principle (San Hsing Kang Ling) laid down by the Lee family, and passed to us from Chan Kam Lee. It is unique within the Chinese Arts, and I have therefore handed it over to our Association for safe-keeping; it is now universally adopted within all clubs of the Association and it is an integral part of their training schedules.

Before you begin, remember that your first priority must always be your own personal defence, and never even think about or plan an attacking movement until you have successfully defended yourself. To do otherwise could be extremely dangerous, until you have had a lot of practice in the art of warding off all types of blows.

First of all we are going to practise our ward-offs from attacks that are aimed at the head, or the chin in particular. If blows are aimed at your face in general, then treat them all the same, and apply the same technique. We mention the chin as simply a target in this early stage, for if something disastrous should happen — like your partner misjudging his reach, or if you did not execute a perfectly timed ward-off, then the chin is the least sensitive point of the face, and therefore no damage should be sustained.

As we have said, this is the system whereby you can put into actual practice your defence requirements, and adapt to any particular situation or variation of attack, without having to stick to a preset code of rules. So that you can get an idea how this can be done let us start you off by telling you what to do. Then, once you have acquired the feel of 'Rolling Away', you can use any of your defence techniques at any time, as you think suitable for that particular situation. First you and your partner should face each other, both in right stance and with your hands in an 'on guard' position, and standing about a yard apart from one another.

1. Your partner steps forward with his right foot, and moves into right Dragon Stance, and as he does so he aims a straight right hand blow at your chin. As the blow comes towards you, move your body back until the weight of your body rests on your rear leg: you should now be in either Cat or Monkey Stance. Now turn your body to the right, swinging your shoulders and, as you do so, bring up your left hand and ward off his blow with a Sun Palm. Sweep his arm past your right shoulder and, as the blow goes harmlessly by, step forward with your right leg, move into Dragon Stance, and aim a straight right hand blow to his chin.

2. As your blow comes towards him, your partner should move his weight onto his rear leg, moving into Cat Stance. He now starts to turn his own shoulders away to his right, and as he does so he brings up his own left hand and wards off your striking arm with his left hand Sun Palm. As your blow is swept past his right shoulder, he now steps forward with his right leg and moves into right Dragon Stance, and again he aims a straight arm right hand blow directly at your chin.

3. As his blow zooms in on its target, again move your weight directly back onto your rear leg, so that you are in right Cat Stance. Turn your shoulders to the left this time, and ward off his blow to your left by using a right hand Sun Palm against his arm, so that his blow passes harmlessly by your left shoulder. Now step forward with your right leg into right Dragon Stance, and once again aim a straight right handed blow, such as the open hand (Chang Shou) or closed fist (Ch'uan T'ou) at his chin.

4. Your partner moves his weight back onto his rear leg as soon as he sees your blow coming at him. As he turns his shoulders to the left he raises his right hand and places his Sun Palm on your arm making your striking unit drift away into space beyond his left shoulder. He now steps forward into right Dragon Stance and aims another straight right blow at your chin.

5. You now move your weight back onto your rear leg, turn your shoulders to your right and raising your left arm this time you execute an arm ward-off, making contact with the little finger edge of your left arm. Step forward into right Dragon Stance and aim another straight blow at his chin, but this time why not make it a Poisoned Hand (Tu Shou) technique?

6. As your blow is delivered, so he moves his weight onto his rear leg, and he can reverse the previous sequence by turning his shoulders to the left. By warding your blow off with his right arm, he ensures that your strike goes by his left side. Now it is his turn to strike again so he moves into his right Dragon Stance as he aims his blow at your face.

In the next few ward-offs, why not try a few of the double hand or double arm techniques? This means that you can bring up both units simultaneously to make an effective shield for yourself; you can utilize two different techniques at the same time — for instance, an arm ward-off with a Sun Palm for ease or convenience; or you can allow one technique to start the ward-off whilst the other arm or hand can finish the sequence of defensive action. This will give you a greater fluidity of movement, and allow you to adjust your defences, not only within a split second, but also quite naturally and quickly to any particular situation that may arise.

7. So, as his blow is executed, you move your weight onto your rear leg and bring both arms upward. Ward off the attack by using both arms together to nullify his attack, and to send his blow to your right by contacting the outside of his arm.

8. Now step forward into your own attack, and aim at his chin. He then moves his weight to his rear leg, and fends off your blow by using an upward arm ward-off, together with a left Sun Palm that follows a fraction behind the arm action, and wards off on the outside of your arm. He then follows through with his own attack.

9. Shift your weight immediately onto your rear leg to increase the range, swing your shoulders to the left, and as you do so bring up both hands simultaneously, to ward off his blow, making contact on the inside of his arm on his forearm. Gently guide it away to your left side. Then step forward into right Dragon Stance, and strike back at him.

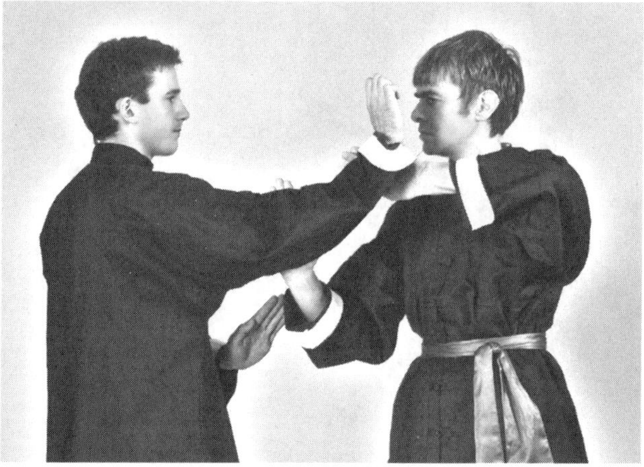

10. Your partner's reflex action will take his weight back onto his rear leg as soon as he sees your blow coming towards him. He will then bring up both hands for his personal defence: why not try a combination of Sun Palm and Cloudy Palm harmonized together, on the outside of your forearm? Then he strikes back at you.

11. After you have taken your body to the rear keep your palms fairly close together as you raise your arms, and come under his forearm to ward off his blow over the top of your head, through the use of a Double Sun Palm Up action.

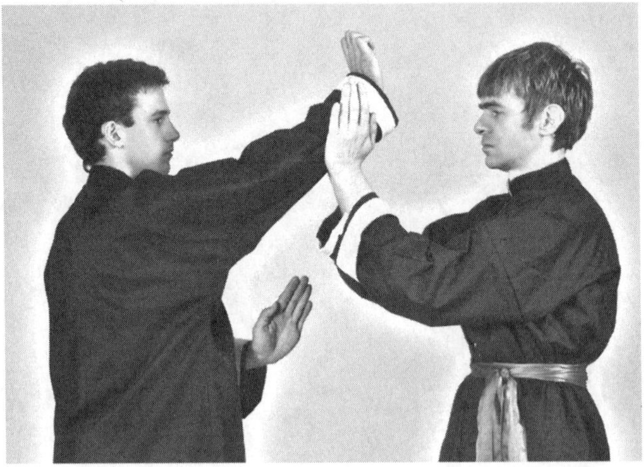

So you can carry on this unique system of attack and defence, each one should take it in turn to put his knowledge into practical application with a real live opponent. You will therefore get first hand experience of the feeling of having blows coming straight at you, and also obtain the instant feel of using your techniques in the personal defence of yourself.

Don't forget to practise all the ward-offs time and time again so that you can start to move instinctively, no matter what angle the blow might come from, and at what force it might be delivered. If you and your partner work in close harmony in this system of training, you will both gain a strong foundation for the vast amount of work that is still to follow.

Once you have attained a good feel of warding blows off away from your chin and face, then start to practise the same system together but this time aim your strikes directly at each other's stomach. Be careful, for the angle of the blow is entirely different, so practise slowly at first so that you can give yourselves time to think about it, adjust to it, and consider what ward-off you want to try. Here are a few ideas:

12. Move your weight back onto your rear leg, and slide the front foot back into Cat Stance, and at the same time turn your body to the left. Then raise your right elbow so that it points at your opponent. Then, keeping your right wrist directly under your elbow, sweep his arm past your left hip. Step forward and aim a straight blow towards his stomach with your right hand.

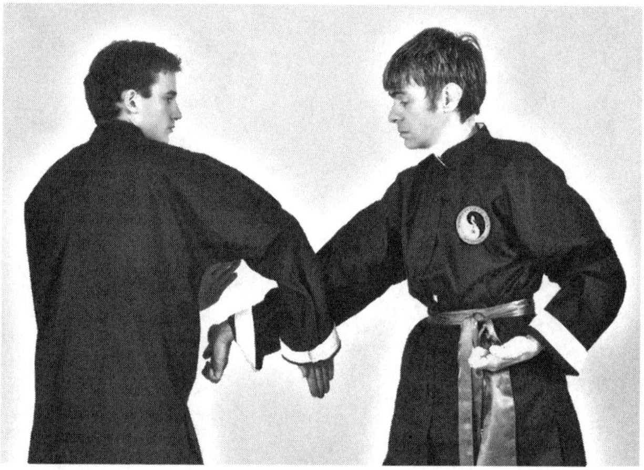

13. Your partner will immediately take his weight back onto his rear leg, pulling his tummy back slightly too. He can then ward off your blow with his right arm, making contact with the outside of your arm on your elbow side, and sweep your blow to his right.

14. As your partner aims his next blow at your stomach, automatically move your weight back onto your rear leg, and ward off his blow with your open left hand to the outside or elbow side of his right arm. Keep all your fingers close together and make sure that they point downwards. Having taken his blow past your right hip, advance into Dragon Stance and strike back.

15. Your partner, seeing your blow coming towards his stomach, will move his weight back onto his rear leg, and bring up his left arm with his elbow pointing directly at you, and his arm hanging down in a Willow Tree ward-off. He makes contact to the elbow side of your arm, and directs your blow past his right hip. Now he will advance and strike back at your stomach.

16. Again without a second thought, move your weight over your rear leg, and as his blow comes within your range, ward it off with your left hand — but this time place it on the inside of his arm, the thumb side, and move his blow past your left hip. Once the danger has been controlled then advance your right leg and strike back at his lower abdomen.

17. He should immediately shift his weight to his rear leg, and this time he could try a Double Sun Palm ward-off to the outside of your right arm on the elbow side, so that the force of your blow is deflected past his right side. But he should take care that all his fingers are kept close together and that they point directly downwards to the floor. Once the deflection is completed, then he once more steps forward and strikes back at you.

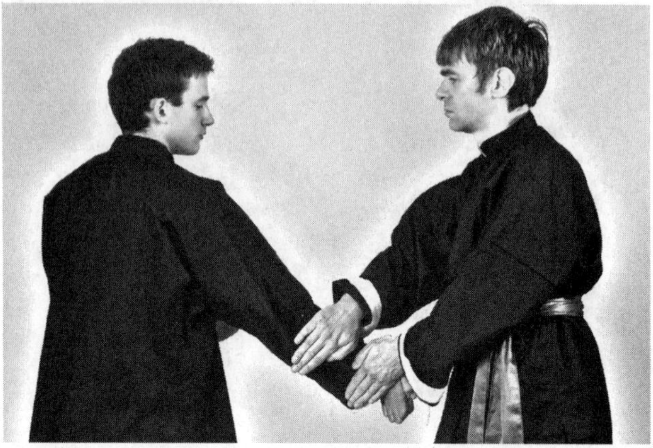

These few movements should help to give you an indication of how you can adopt this unique system of training to acquire the benefits and insight of the vast field of ward-offs and parries, and will enable you to practise every technique and movement under a very harmonious and happy atmosphere with a friend. So when the time comes (and let us hope it never arrives) that you have to practise self-defence in reality, then you will have had the enormous experience of meeting all possible contingencies before they actually arrive, and your preparation will have been proved well worthwhile.

Don't forget, that whilst practising this roll-away system that you try every type of ward-off and parry, on the inside and the outside of the arm, so that you can acquire the skill so necessary in an unexpected situation, and can react within a split second, and can do the correct thing at the right moment. All this does depend on an instinctive reflex, as do all techniques in Feng Shou kung fu, so practise very slowly at first. In this way you will have time to think, time to watch out for your own mistakes, time to correct any faults, time to watch the weaknesses in your partner's stances, time to see the openings for a counter action, and time to gain sufficient experience in all these.

All these techniques are extremely important, especially where there is no Feng Shou Master or Feng Shou club near to you, so that you can watch and learn, and be guided through the initial stages. You will have to learn to correct yourself, and remember at all times to keep soft, inwardly and externally. Softness starts within yourself, and no one can tell you how it feels; it is only something that you can acquire. Unfortunately it is easy to get harder and harder, without realizing it, so you will have to make a special effort to watch out that you are not becoming stiff and tense, for this would be found to be a handicap when you meet members of our association. Even one second lost somewhere within a technique or evasion movement could mean that you might be caught with a counter technique. So once again, let us remind you to: KEEP SOFT.

Your natural movement, combined with our dynamic techniques, will enable you to have an effective as well as a practical skill. Eventually you will learn to 'feel' your opponent's intentions through the medium of hand and arm contact, and this will give you an enormous advantage.

Later on, such will be your hyper-sensitivity that you will be able to execute our roll-away system completely blindfolded, as our higher grades are expected to do. When you get to this stage then your 'feel' becomes extremely acute, so that you can feel your opponent's intentions without being in physical contact with him whatsoever. Let this be one of your ultimate aims.

Chapter 11

Evasion Exercises

Evasion does not mean running half a mile away from the source of trouble, and nor does it mean putting your hands over your ears and your head into the sand; it means that by moving lightly and swiftly away from the angle of attack, the blow, strike, kick or weapon thrust will miss its objective. In so doing you will have placed yourself in such a position that you are able to strike back instantly, with accurate precision and complete awareness of the immediate situation, yet still retain a perfect balance.

This is where the constant practice of the stances comes in very useful in both your attack and your defence, for they will take you in reach or out of range depending on the attitude that you wish to adopt at the time, and based upon your own immediate reaction. But everything will depend on your own personal versatility, including the knowledge and experience of evading an attack through the correct movement of your legs, body and even your head. This is where your experience of learning to move from one stance to another will be valuable and create the wonderful foundation on which to build the vast field of the Feng Shou evasion techniques.

One of the golden rules of our evasion exercises is that whilst you may move out of the way of an attack, you should also try to ensure that at the same time you are in range of your opponent with your own striking units so that you are able to counter. However, this will depend upon the circumstances at the time, and of course, it may not always be possible. However, you will appreciate the advantages and disadvantages of each situation as your own experience increases through your own personal training. So ensure that you practise constantly and continuously. It is no good training intensively for seven days, then laying off for a month: it is much better to set aside regular days and times each week, so that your training can be kept up regularly. Then you will obtain the maximum benefit from your regular practice and dedication.

Whilst you can practice the moves in front of a mirror at home, it will be much better to practise with a friend, or join a Feng Shou club, if there happens to be one in your locality. But remember, whenever you practise our evasions, that you should always try to be out of range of your opponent's blow, yet you should always be in range with one of your own weapons. This is very important and one of our golden rules.

There are three main evasion exercises or forms in the art of Feng Shou. These are:

1. The Clock Face (Chung Mien)
2. The Tea Cup (Ch'a Pei)
3. The Five Lotus Petals (Wu Lien Huapan)

Each one has a completely different routine, and each conforms to certain principles which will enable you to defend yourself from varying angles of attack, once you have learnt to do the sequence or routine movement of each exercise.

It is essential however, that you practise these exercises constantly, day in and day out, because evasion should be your number one priority whether you are weak or strong. In the soft arts of China, and our Feng Shou art is possibly one of the softest of the soft, the high speeds that are maintained throughout give you very little time to stop and think. Reactions must be spontaneous and the movements have to be very fast indeed and executed instinctively. Practise slowly in the beginning, and in so doing ensure that your balance is as perfect as you can get it, that you maintain your weight on the correct leg, and keep your body upright without tension or stiffness. Always keep your hands in an 'on guard' position so that they can be used, if necessary, within a split second.

Whilst these can be practised on your own it is most essential to have a friend or partner with whom you can practise because it is important that you react correctly, and also you will get used to a hand or fist coming directly at your face or your body. This will not only get you accustomed to being under attack, even though you and your friend will be working in a friendly harmonious atmosphere, but helps you to appreciate the angles of the blows, and increases the speed of your thought, reactions, and physical movement.

The Clock Face (Chung Mien)

Basic Set

You and your partner stand at an arm's length in front of each other and ask your partner to step directly forward into a right Dragon Stance (Lung Shih), and as he does so he must aim a straight arm open hand blow directly at your chin.

1. As the blow comes towards you, step directly back with your left leg, and put about ninety per cent of your weight on to it, bending the left knee slightly. At the same time turn your right toes to the left, and also turn the body so that it faces to the left. You should now be in Leopard Stance and this is the stance that you will move into in all our Clock Face evasion movements. As you maintain the majority of your weight on your left leg, ensure that you keep your body upright.

Both you and your partner now move back to the original starting position. He does this by moving his right foot back, and you move your left foot forward till it is alongside your right foot, turning your body to the right slightly so that you once again face your partner, and you will find yourself back to the neutral starting point.

2. As he moves forward again into right Dragon Stance, and strikes again at your chin, this time step diagonally back with your left leg, bending the left knee and placing your body weight upon it. Then both of you move back to your starting positions.

3. Again he steps forward and strikes at your chin. Now you must step directly to your left, repeating the action for Leopard Stance by bending the left knee and placing your body weight on to the left leg. Then once again you both retire to your neutral starting position.

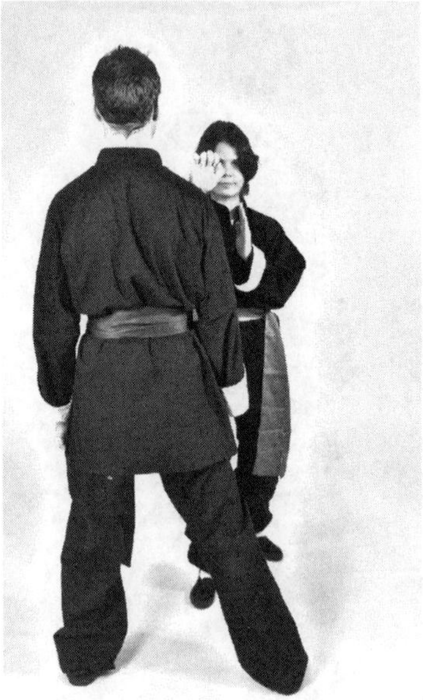

4. He strikes once more as he steps into his Dragon Stance. This time you step diagonally forward with your left foot, placing your weight upon it and bending the left knee, but this time also turn your shoulders to the right, so that you are parallel with your partner's arm. Then you once again return to the neutral starting point, and your partner does the same.

5. As he strikes at your chin again, this time you step diagonally forward with your right foot, bending the right knee and placing your weight onto the right leg. Turn your shoulders to the left so that you once again face your partner's arm. Then return back to the starting position.

6. He strikes at you once more, and you now step directly to your right with your right foot, bending your right knee, and placing your weight onto the right leg. Then you both return to your starting positions.

7. Once again he aims a blow at your chin and this time you step diagonally backwards with your right foot, placing your weight upon it as you bend your right knee. Turn your body slightly to the right, and also turn your left foot a little to your right, so that you are in a correct Leopard Stance. Both of you now return to your starting positions.

8. As the eighth blow comes towards you, turn your body to the right, and step back a pace with your right foot, bending the right knee, and placing your body weight onto your right leg. Correct the angle of your left foot by moving your left toes to your right. Now you both return to the neutral starting position.

That is the basic sequence of the eight evasion movements of the Clock Face and now it is your turn to strike towards your partner's chin, and he will move into those eight different directions, ensuring that he evades your blow as you have just done.

Both of you must practise these over and over again until all your movements become light, flexible, supple and fast. Once you have acquired this dexterity, lightness and swiftness, then try the next stage.

Alternative Striking

Both of you must practise the same sequence of the eight basic movements, but this time you alternate your striking and your evasion like this:

(i) Your partner strikes, and you move into position No. 1, and then you both move back to the starting positions.
(ii) Now this time you strike at your partner, and he moves into position No. 1, and then you both move back to your starting positions.
(iii) He now strikes at you, and you move into position No. 2, and then you both return to the neutral position.
(iv) Now you strike at your partner, and he moves into position No. 2 and you both go back to the starting positions.

This goes on until the basic eight directions of evasion have been accomplished smoothly and without fault. Don't let up with your training, and practise it time and time again until you have every movement perfect, fluent, smooth, soft and speedy.

It is also a very good idea to reverse the complete sequence and practise it in an anti-clockwise direction, so that you start with your right foot movements, then follow them with your left foot movements for the last four directions. This will help to build up your flexibility, to the left and to the right.

Having really conquered this stage, then we can go on to the next stage of progression, using the same evasion exercise.

Advanced Alternative Striking

This third stage incorporates the alternative striking principle, but this time you evade each other's blows by stepping out in any of the eight directions as you choose. Whilst you step to any of the prescribed eight directions, you do not have to work to the pre-arranged sequence. Do not jump too quickly into this stage, make absolutely sure that you have the two previous stages off perfectly first, then this stage will hold no handicaps, and you will find it quite easy to do.

Fourth Stage: Rollaways
Once you have conquered the previous three stages, and can now move lightly whilst still maintaining your balance at all times, then, and only then, should you start to practise this stage which you can call 'alternative striking *but* from the new position', wherever the new position might be. Not only do you strike from the new position that you have stepped into by evading his blow, but instead of keeping to the format of the Clock Face, you can now move and strike from any of those eight positions. In other words, once you move into your evasion, irrespective of the angle created by your own personal movement, you now strike at your partner from the position that you have chosen. Your partner must, in turn, move into any one of the eight positions or angles, to evade your strike.

The Tea Cup (Ch'a Pei)

Basic Set
Both you and your partner stand in right Snake Stance. To start this evasion exercise, he steps forward with his right foot into right Dragon Stance, and as he steps he aims a straight blow directly at your chin. As the blow comes towards you so you start this new sequence of evasion movements.

1. Move your left leg forward, turning your body to the right whilst you are executing these two moves, move your right leg back so that your chest is now parallel to the outside of your partner's arm. Once you are squarely placed by the side of his arm, you should now be in Bear Stance with your weight evenly distributed on both legs.

As your partner pulls his arm back and his body to the neutral starting position, now is the time for you to return to your own starting point, and you do this by moving your feet in a preset sequence. The right foot moves first, back to the original spot in your starting position. As it moves you turn your body to the left, and as you transfer your weight onto your right leg, you then withdraw your left foot so that you can replace it on the original spot.

Move No. 1

Move No. 2

The Tea Cup - Neutral Position

Move No. 3

Move No. 4

2. Your partner once more steps forward and aims another blow straight at your chin, and this time you move your right foot forward, turning your shoulders to the left. As soon as your weight moves on to your right leg, you step back with your left foot so that both feet are now side by side in Bear Stance. Your chest and shoulders are square to your partner's arm, but this time you are facing the inside position of his arm.

As he withdraws back to his starting position, you also commence your return journey back to your neutral starting position, by moving your left leg first, turning your shoulders to the right, then withdrawing your right foot back alongside your left foot.

3. Your partner strikes again, and this time you step back with your right foot, turning your body and shoulders to the right. Then withdraw your left foot so that you are once again standing square and facing the outside of your opponent's arm, but this time you are beyond the range of his hand, and it will seem to be a long, long way from you. He then withdraws back to his starting position, and you follow his withdrawal by turning your shoulders to the left, step forward with your left foot, then follow it with your right foot, and you should be back in your original starting position.

4. He steps forward again and strikes once more at your chin, and this time you turn your shoulders to the left, step diagonally back with your left foot, and let the right foot automatically follow so that you stand once more square to your opponent's arm, but a long way out of reach. As he withdraws to his neutral position, you turn your body back to the right, stepping first with the right foot, then follow it with the left foot, so that you are once more back in the starting position.

Alternative Striking

Before commencing this second stage, make sure that you practise the basic sequence time and time again, so that the feet can move very lightly and smoothly across the surface of the floor, just as if you were floating on air. Ensure that you retain your balance at all times, especially when you are turning your shoulders at the same time as you move your feet. Don't take too big a step, just allow the foot to lift about an inch off the floor, as you glide from one position to another. This will, as you will find out, builds up a very high speed of movement. Practise this continuously until both you and your partner have acquired a smooth, flowing action and a very fast evasion. Once you have accomplished this, then try this next stage.

1. As your opponent strikes, you move off into the No. 1 position, then he goes back to the neutral position, and you move back to your own starting position as well. Now this time it is your turn to strike and as you do so he moves into position No. 1. Then you both move back to your own starting positions.

2. Now this time, as your opponent strikes towards your chin, you move into position No. 2, then afterwards you both go back from whence you came. Then you step forward and strike at his chin, and he floats away to position No. 2, and then you both move back to the neutral locality.

3. It is now his turn to strike once more and, as he does so, you now move into position No. 3, and once the evasion has been completed you both go back to the starting position. You now strike, and he turns away into the third sequence, and afterwards you both go back to the point of starting.

4. Your opponent strikes, and you now move into the fourth position of the Tea Cup set, and having completed the evasion, both you and your opponent move back to the starting position. As soon as you get there, you step forward into Dragon Stance and strike at his chin, and without hesitation he turns away into position No. 4. You then both return to the neutral starting position.

To reiterate, you should practise the Tea Cup evasion sequence and the alternative striking time and time again until you obtain a smooth, flowing and floating movement from one stance to the other, ensuring that there is no time lag between one change and another. Remember too, that as your hands and arms can move easily at your will, then let your feet and your body move just as naturally, because Feng Shou is that kind of art. It is one of the fastest arts of China, and dexterity, flexibility, suppleness and speed are essential requirements, but it takes time, perseverance and dedication over a long period to reach the high standard and the perfection which we all aim for in our endeavour to follow the TAO of our lives.

Advanced Alternative Striking

This, the third stage of the Tea Cup, is only a slight advancement of the alternative striking principle. All that is necessary is to move to any of the four positions, as your partner strikes at you, and he will do the same when you strike at him.

When you get to this stage it will not be necessary for you to stick to the prescribed format or sequence; you can please yourself to which position you would like to go, but make sure that you do move into them all, so that you can get used to the angles that are involved.

Fourth Stage: Roll-aways

Once you have acquired the flexibility of moving through the alternative striking sequences without loss of time, or hesitation, and returning smoothly back to the starting position, then you are ready to start the next stage which is to strike from any of the positions that you may have moved into on your evasion.

At first, you may find this a little different because of the angles involved, for they are more acute. In addition, when you move to the left front or the left rear, you will find it easier to strike from a left Dragon Stance, and also to strike with your left hand. When you move to the right then you will find it better to strike with the right hand and from a right Dragon Stance.

So therefore you will be achieving quite a number of techniques, not only striking from a new position and a new angle, but you will also be learning to execute your technique with alternative hands and stances.

Once again let us advise you to practise very slowly, get used to the new angles of attack, the feel of floating into a different position, and the entirely different appreciation of spotting which arm he is going to attack with. Don't forget that when you practise our roll-away system, you do not have to adhere to the sequence as laid down. You can evade in any one of those four directions in the split second that you have, from the time he starts to swing his blow at you.

The Five Lotus Petals (Wu Lien Huapan)

Basic Set

The method of this evasion exercise is the continual use of the body and head, with just a few movements of the feet, but it is on the flexibility of the body that this dynamic evasion sequence concentrates its main endeavours. However, let us give you a serious warning: make sure that your body is really flexible before you start this set, by ensuring that the limbering exercises are carried out daily, for in this set your opponent's blow may only be a matter of one or two inches away from your head, chest or waist. So make absolutely sure that your evasion technique is really good, and don't attempt this evasion exercise until you are certain that you have the necessary flexibility and the confidence.

Your partner will adopt the right Snake Stance ready to execute his strikes by moving into his right Dragon Stance. You stand in Bear Stance about a yard (metre) in front of your partner.

1. Step directly to the left with your left foot, bending your left knee, and putting your weight onto your left leg. You are now in Leopard Stance, as your partner steps forward and strikes at your chin. Then you both return to your neutral starting position.

2. As your partner throws his next blow at your chin, move into right Leopard Stance by stepping directly to your right with the right foot, bending your right knee, and putting the majority of weight onto your right leg. Then you both move back to your starting positions.

3. As the third blow comes towards you, step to your left with your left foot. Then allow your right foot to slice sideways in the same direction, until both feet are about the width of your shoulders apart, and you will find yourself in our Bear Stance. As your partner moves back to his starting position, you do too, by moving the right leg first, then follow it with your left.

4. Your partner next throws his fourth blow at you, and as you see it coming, move your right foot directly to your right, and draw your left foot in the same direction immediately afterwards, so that both feet are apart but parallel in the Bear Stance. As your partner retires, move back to your neutral spot by moving your left foot first, then follow it with your right foot.

From now on watch out, for the feet do not move at all, and only the body and the head move to execute the evasion techniques which are involved.

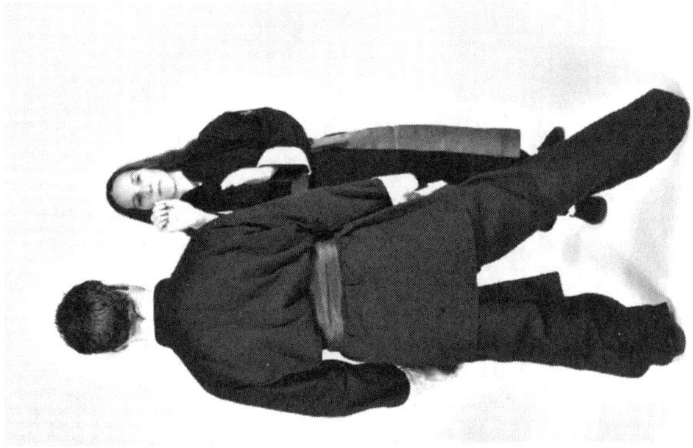

The Five Lotus Petals - Move No. 1

Nuetral Position

Move No. 2

Move No. 3

Neutral Position

Move No. 4

Move No. 5

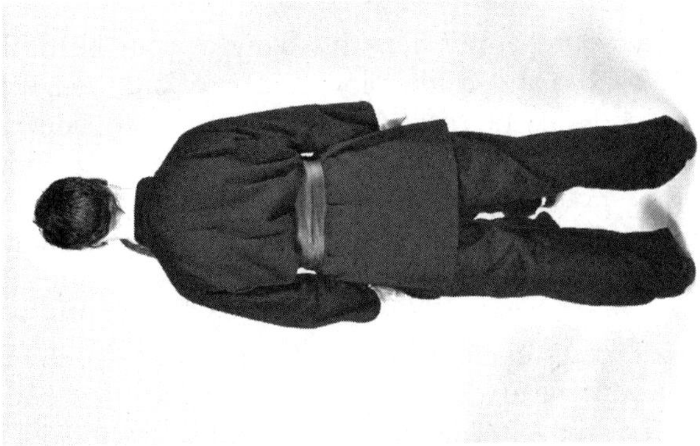

Neutral Position

Move No. 6

5. Now as your opponent strikes at your chin, without moving your feet, turn your shoulders to the right, throwing the majority of your weight onto your left leg and allowing your right hip to move slightly back too. Ensure that your chest is parallel to your opponent's arm, and this movement will allow his blow to pass harmlessly in front of your chest and chin. Your partner returns to his starting position, and all you have to do to return to your original stance is to simply unwind by turning to your left.

6. Next, as your partner's blow comes towards you, swing your shoulders to the left, placing most of your weight on to your right leg, and also turn the hips to the left as well, allowing the blow to pass harmlessly in front of your chest and chin. By the way, what stance should this be? Lion Stance, of course. Now you both return back to your starting positions.

7. This time your partner aims his blow at your head, in the region of your nose and, as the blow comes towards you, without moving the body or the feet, just throw your head sideways to the left, so that his hand will pass over your right shoulder, between the shoulder and the right side of your face. As he withdraws his arm to move back to his starting position, just straighten your head.

8. He now throws another blow straight at your face, and this time throw your head directly to your right, so that his blow passes between the left side of your face and your shoulder. Now you both return to your neutral position.

9. This time your partner will aim his blow at your stomach, and as the hand comes towards its target, you now move into Leopard Stance, without moving the feet at all. All you do is to thrust your hips directly sideways to the right, bending your shoulders slightly to your left, so that the weight of your body is mainly on your right leg, and his blow should pass harmlessly by your left hip and under your left arm. As he pulls his arm back to return to his starting position, you straighten your body, and you too are back to your original position.

10. Your partner now throws another blow at your stomach, and this time you throw your hips to the left, whilst leaning very slightly to your right. You will find that again his blow will miss,

Move No. 7

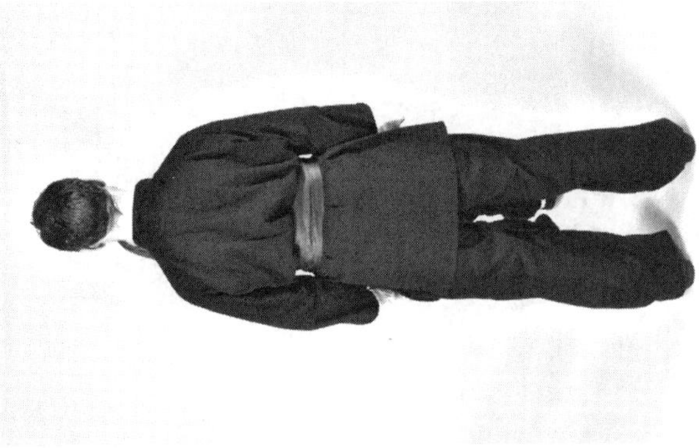

Neutral Position

Move No. 8

Move No. 9

Neutral Position

Move No. 10

and pass by your right hip. He then pulls back to his neutral position, and you just have to straighten your body once more.

There is a lot of work in this sequence, and because the range of his strike may be only a few inches away from your head, body or hips, you have got to ensure that your evasion technique is perfect, and that all your movements are synchronized accurately. You must learn to react within a split second. So practise this evasion exercise over and over again, until you have each movement fulfilled smoothly and perfectly.

In all our clubs, no matter what part of the world this art is practised, you will find that all these basic evasions are executed at every training session, irrespective of how good the person might be or how long he has been practising the art. They will still repeat these basics every lesson, to try and attain perfection in footwork, body movement, balance and split-second reaction.

Alternative Striking

This is again executed on the principles of the other two previous exercises. First your partner will strike and you move into the first position. Then, having returned to the starting position, it is your turn to strike, and he then moves into the position of the first evasion.

He now strikes again and you move into position No. 2, and then you both automatically return to your starting points. You strike and he moves in position No. 2, then both go back to the neutral point. So you will both carry on, taking it in turns to strike, going right through all the evasion exercises, both to the left and to the right, until the synchronization of all the movements have become perfect or as perfect as you can get them.

Third Stage — Roll-aways

Approach this stage with extreme caution; and practise very, very slowly, striking from your new position; sometimes you will move either with the one step or the two step evasions, and at other times you will not move at all, but just resort to the utilization of your bodies or your heads. Make absolutely sure that you both take it in turns to execute the strike, and naturally from any new position that you might adopt.

Once again, we must emphasize that you must practise

slowly, and really get accustomed to these very close evasions. In this way you won't have the embarrassment of accidentally striking your partner, who, after all, is there to help you (and you can help him too), to get used to these new angles of attack, the type of blow that is being delivered, and the various target areas that may present themselves.

But these evasions are just the beginning of many more to come, for each set has a further eight extensions, So there is a lot of work lying ahead, but when you get to this point in this book you will have passed the first hurdle.

Chapter 12

Ch'i Shou — The Adhering Hand

Never be mistaken about Feng Shou kung fu: it is a dynamic and very devastating art, exceedingly fast with great dexterity and suppleness, and that is one of the reasons why we do not allow sparring sessions to take place amongst the student grades. In such a specialized art as this, where women can strike as hard as ten men when they use the power of Ch'i, it takes time to gain sufficient experience with the thousands of techniques that are involved.

Training in the sparring aspects only starts with the Masters or Teachers who have sufficient number of years in the practice of this art to have mastered the many techniques that are required for proficiency. Even so they are taken through this section in very easy training sessions, paying particular attention to every section, such as speed, distance, high and low blows, footwork, evasion techniques, and maximum body control of yourself and also of your opponent.

However, this policy does not entirely exclude you from the enjoyment of matching your skill against an opponent, in a friendly form of combat and a battle of wits, technique and experience.

Ch'i Shou is, in a wide sense, an exercise in complete submission, in a multitude of ways, and yet, in giving way to force, you win. There must be no resistance whatsoever, either in mind, body or energy, and you must learn to give way to every grain of pressure that your opponent may exert against you. The ultimate aim is to turn his power, strength and weight back against himself.

For instance, if you are in a wrist-to-wrist contact with an opponent who leads at you with his right arm, yield completely and at the same time turn your body to your right, so that his arm goes past your right shoulder. He is now pushing, not at you personally, but pushing nothing but the air. At the maximum point of his reach, his balance will begin to feel a bit shaky, and the weight of his body will have moved onto his toes. If you can continue to keep him going in the same direction, by pushing gently with your left hand as well, then he will fall over, no matter how big he might be.

That is simply the whole essence of Ch'i Shou, and the very soft art of Feng Shou: completely utilizing your opponent's force, aggression, and balance against himself, thereby assisting him to create his own downfall. This will apply at all times, and under all circumstances and in every situation, no matter how tall or how heavy or even how strong he might be, for the foundation of good balance must rest entirely on the feet and the legs.

If you happen to push your partner from behind, you will notice his weight will automatically move forward, and to try to maintain adequate balance he will grip with his toes to try and stay upright. If you push him from the front, he has nothing on his heels to grip with, and so he cannot maintain or recover his equilibrium, for there is nothing there to help provide the leverage necessary for him to retain an upright stature. Through your influence and technique, therefore, he will either have to step back or fall backwards.

If he should step back to regain his balance, or if you can so arrange or manipulate the situation so that he has to step back, you can still apply that light and gentle pushing action that will hold his balance over his heels. You can therefore topple him over, even with the pressure of one of your fingers.

Always remember, no matter how you stand, and whatever stance you may adopt, there is a minimum of fifty per cent weakness. In fact, no matter what stance you may acquire, you will always have six points of weakness: to your left, to your right, backward, forward, downwards and upwards. This will always apply to any posture or stance that may be used by your opponent. Therefore, knowing which way to push or to coax your opponent to move into, will take time and experience, and there is no better way of learning to do this than through the constant practice of Ch'i Shou.

But before you begin to practise this art, you must be completely relaxed in mind, body and spirit, and at all times be one with yourself. To achieve this, you may find it helpful to do a short session of the breathing exercises that we mention in this book.

The real point about Ch'i Shou is that you have to be in a peaceful state of mind so that you are aware of the feel of the slightest movement, and sensitive enough to register the most minute shift in emphasis. You must be conscious of the delicate balance that exists within everything, together with the understanding of the amount of force that is being applied against you, and also have a deep appreciation of the skill of your opponent.

You must learn to yield to every type of force that your opponent may exert against you, whether it is physical, energy, mental or weight, although all this may only come through constant practice and a lot of practical experience. So initially both of you should try to move very slowly using only the barest minimum of pressure.

At first, giving way with no resistance whatsoever may seem to be against your whole concept of fighting, and therefore you may find this quite difficult to achieve. Nevertheless, you should try and persevere, because no matter how strong you are, there is always someone stronger, taller, and heavier than you, whose force you cannot oppose. So you must learn to channel your opponent's strength, power, weight and balance and to turn them all against himself. These are the basic principles behind Ch'i Shou, for if you try to use physical force and very fast movements, in the end you will have achieved nothing, learnt nothing, felt nothing, and you will find that you have also attained nothing from all of your work.

You already understand that one of the greatest values in practising Ch'i Shou is that it will help you to appreciate and be more conscious of the balance of the body, not only your opponent's, but also your own. But another equally important aspect of Ch'i Shou is being able to counter any of your opponent's intended moves, before he actually can make them. This is not mind reading or clairvoyance, it is the intuition and understanding that you acquire through your experience in this art.

If you practise enough, you will be able to do this as well, just like any other Feng Shou expert. In a way it might be referred to as a sixth sense, but it is more than this really, for through your diligent practise you do become hyper-sensitive, and very much aware of the meaning of all of your opponent's movements, no matter how little or how gentle they might be.

Over a period of time, this hyper-sensitivity develops to such a degree that you will eventually 'feel' an opponent, even though you may not see him or hear him, and this feeling is so precise that you will be able to tell which arm or leg will be used if he tries to attack you.

In order to make yourself more receptive to this kind of inner development you must start adhering to the natural order of the universe, commence eating the Ch'ang Ming (Taoist Long Life Therapy) way, then work diligently so that you can build up within yourself the channels of receptivity, and then through the training of Ch'i Shou you will slowly attain a state of super-sensitivity. If you don't live this way then you can so easily miss the tiny revealing signs that can tell you so much. In addition, your own touch must be as delicate as possible or it can blur the sensation of what your opponent is doing, or what he is intending to do.

This lightness of touch cannot be over-emphasized. It must be so fine that if a feather fell on your arm, it would slowly yield beneath the weight of it. In the same way, you and your partner ought to yield to each other's technique and pressure.

At all times you must be in an arm or hand contact with your opponent and then you will find that, after a while, even if you close your eyes, you will be able to tell whether his weight is on the rear leg or the front foot, if he leans slightly too much in one direction or even if he should move the other hand or arm.

You will pick up these changes not only through your sensitivity and very strong concentration, but also through those infinitesimal variations that exist in the angles of approach, the levels of pressure and those minute muscular movements which will give him and his intentions away, and reveal to you the complete story.

When you have conquered the basics of the techniques, and have understood the principles involved, you will find yourself advancing very quickly, for there are so many variations of movements within movements that you will be able to ad lib many sequences that may suit your build, your attitude at the time, even your own favourite side, plus the depth of your sensitivity. But don't try and run before you can walk! Start with the following short sequence, and build on it as you slowly progress.

Both you and your partner stand facing one another in right Snake Stance, with both knees slightly bent and your back nice and straight. Raise your right hand so that the back of your right wrist lightly touches the back of your partner's right wrist: this is the contact that you want to maintain throughout this exercise.

Now your partner starts to move his arm gently forward as if to press you back. Immediately you feel that extra pressure, give way to his force, by transferring your weight on to your rear leg. Then, when you consider that he has reached the limit of his balance, turn to one side, thus leaving him in a very unstable position, for he is leaning forward against nothing, pushing only the thin air.

Now that the forward pressure has been diverted away, by the action of your arm and body, you can utilize his own force and power against himself. Without breaking contact, float his arm in

Step 1

Step 2

front of your chest, and then take it out to your right, and circle it back to a point where you can lightly touch his chest or his left shoulder with the back of his own arm. At this point you will be able to topple him or, as we call it in our arts, you have uprooted his balance.

However, if his reaction is good, or his balance is fundamentally stable, or your timing is not perfect, then it is quite possible that he will manage to stay upright and maintain his balance. Then he too can lean slightly back and transfer his weight correctly, and ride your slight pressure on his arm by turning his body to his right. Then he will be able to exploit the same advantage against your own movement and your weight distribution.

What a simple movement this is, that you have worked out with your partner! When you have mastered the feel of it, then carry on a little further. Learning to utilize both arms so that they can absorb a slight pressure from any angle that your opponent may move your arms into, whether it be high or low. Remember that your feet, at this particular stage, should remain firm and stationary on the floor. If you have to move them at all, even by the slightest movement, then your balance has been upset, and that is one up to your partner.

It is important to be able to use both sides of the body with equal dexterity, and with as near equal skill as is possible. So both you and your partner change your stance, and practise this movement also in the left style. Once you have mastered the movements through the use of one hand and arm, then try using both hands. When you do this you will find that the possibilities of variation, angles, pressure and changes in style and balance which are open to you are infinite, for not only can you uproot your partner forwards, backwards, left, right, downwards (which is pretty hard to do), and also upwards whereby your partner's feet actually leave the floor, which is the hardest or most difficult technique to accomplish, of all.

These last two movements will be learnt much later. For the time being, stick to the basic principles, and take note of the following rules and guidelines which you will find extremely useful through the early stages of your progression.

1. Make sure that if you change hands at any time one hand or arm is always in contact with your partner's arm.
2. Whilst you can have both hands touching him simultaneously, only one hand should actually be doing the

work. If both hands work at the same time, we call this 'double weighting', and you can very easily be uprooted. So if at any time you have two hands touching, make the period of contact as short as possible.

3. Utilize the full scope of your hands, arms and body to cover every conceivable angle of defence and countering movements.
4. If you want to move forward, then you will find it easier if you move your body back first. Similarly, if you want to move to your right, then go to the left first, and so on. In other words, before you move towards any direction move a little first in the opposite direction. Try it, and you will slowly understand why, for it not only increases your leverage by giving additional space for your arms and hands, and eventually with your footwork, but it also takes advantage of your opponent's normal physical reactions.
5. Never 'double weight' because this is a pointless expenditure of your energy, and creates weaknesses within yourself. It is far better to have your energy flowing out of only one hand at a time, while the other rests lightly on your opponent.
6. For much the same reason, avoid putting your weight on both legs at the same time. This 'double weighting' of your balance also has the tendency to weaken your stance, and if your partner is sensitive enough he will be able to feel it, and so he will find comparatively simple to uproot you.

Ch'i Shou may seem a very passive form of combat to you, and, at this stage in your training, may seem to hold no meaning whatsoever, and you may even think that as a form of fighting it is virtually useless. That is where you would be wrong, and very wrong indeed. Hidden within its depth is the development of your potential inner self. These sensitive internal areas are so subtle that only through a medium as delicate as Ch'i Shou can you hope to grasp their fundamental meanings, practicalities, and gentle indescribable changes. In addition, it is the nearest thing to close quarter fighting that you will ever come across, and therefore it is invaluable to you in your training.

So don't neglect this part of your training, for the whole of the Chinese arts were born around it.

Chapter 13

Tu Shou — Poison Hand Form

By now you have covered many basic aspects of Feng Shou kung fu, and have practised them to such an extent that if anyone did attack you, you could prove to be quite a formidable opponent, no matter what kind of situation might arise.

You can ward-off almost any type of attack, and with your experience turn it in such a way that you will gain the advantage with complete simplicity. Similarly, you know how to use your feet and your body in the skilful art of evasion; you know how to use your hands in the various forms of striking, and the best areas to strike at, for quick results.

However, Feng Shou is such a comprehensive art that you can go on learning the vast range of techniques for ever, as well as developing the crucial weaknesses within yourself, attaining perfection in movement, gaining the necessary experience, increasing speeds, and learning to live constantly in accordance to the laws of the universe and our personal Tao.

Speed is something that can improve through constant practice, and it needs concentration, arm and body control, for you can never be too fast. Therefore, to help you gain extra speed and control of your hands and arms, we have a number of very ancient sets of movements, in one of our 'forms', which is called the 'Poison Hand Form' (Tu Shou).

These sets incorporate a series of defensive arm and leg movements, which are always practised very softly, slowly and gently. However, these sets also include a number of hand and leg strikes which must all be practised regularly, so that you can gradually build them up into lightning-fast striking actions, harmonized with high speed changes in the various striking units that we use.

Tu Shou therefore, was primarily designed by our Taoist

masters, as a high-speed hand training with the ultimate aim of enabling you to strike at various targets with the speed of lightning. Tu Shou consists of fourteen different sets of movements in all, but we will only explain the first three sets of this form in this book. You will find them fairly easy to learn as they all have the same sequence and the only changes that makes one set different from the others is the three hand strikes which are incorporated into each one.

First Set of Tu Shou

Starting Position: Riding Horse Stance (Ch'i Ma Shih)

1. Step back one pace with your right foot, and place your body weight onto your right leg, and you should be in Monkey Stance. At the same time as you step back, make an upward left arm ward-off. Make sure that your right hand with palm facing upward is kept close to your right waistline.

2. Step forward with your right leg, so that it is one pace ahead of your left foot. Move your weight onto your right leg so that you are now in Dragon Stance, with your rear leg firm and straight. At the same time as you step forward, bring your left hand back to your left side with the palm of the hand up, and throw your right arm round in a big circle in a hand sword strike, palm up, to the left side neck of an imaginary opponent.

3. Stay in your right Dragon Stance. Now direct your left hand spear, in a straight forward arm thrust, to your opponent's heart. At the same time as your left arm moves forward pull your right hand back, palm up, alongside your right waistline.

4. Stay in your right Dragon Stance and pull your left hand back to your left side waistline with the left palm facing upward; meanwhile, your right arm shoots directly forward with your right hand spear aiming directly at your imaginary opponent's heart.
5. Execute a left arm upward ward-off and, as you do so, bring

your body weight back onto your left leg, with your left knee bent slightly, and also withdraw your right foot, keeping the right toes in touch with the floor, so that you are in right Cat Stance.

6. Lift your right foot into the air, and make a front snap kick

directly forward, imagining that the target you are aiming for is your opponent's groin.

8. Now move your right foot forward until it is on a level with

7. Swing your right leg down and step back one pace with your right foot to the rear of your left foot, keeping your front foot flat on the floor. You should now be in a Monkey Stance. As you step back, swing both arms upward, in front of your body until they both cross in front of the head and on a level with your forehead.

Then, without stopping your flow of movement, bring both of your arms straight down the centre line of your body, to stop in front of the lower stomach. At this stage both arms separate and sweep to the outside of your own thighs.

your left foot, and bend both knees. You are now back in the Riding Horse Stance. Simultaneously, both arms are brought inward and upward until they nestle close to your waistline on either side of your body. The palms of the hands should face upwards, with the hands clenched into fists.

That now completes the first half of this first set.
Nos. 9 to 16

This is exactly the same sequence of movements as before, the only difference being that this time you practise to the left side — in other words you reverse all the movements. So instead of stepping back with your right foot, you step back with your left, and instead of warding-off with the left arm you ward-off with your right, and so on.

Second Set of Tu Shou

1. This movement is exactly the same as No. 1 in the First Set.

2. Same as No. 2 of the First Set, but as you step into right Dragon Stance you throw a right Hammer Fist (Ch'uan Ch'ui) to your opponent's left temple.

3. This is a left handed Two Finger Spear (Liang Chih Ch'iang) to your opponent's eyes.

4. This is now a right Hand Spear to your opponent's heart.

5. Same as No. 5 in the First Set.

6. Same as No. 6 in the First Set.

7. Same as No. 7 in the First Set.

8. Same as No. 8 in the First Set.

Nos. 9 to 16 are the same as above but again they are now executed on the left side.

Third Set of Tu Shou

1. This is the same as No. 1 in the First Set.

2. The body movements are the same as No. 2 in the First Set, but as you step into the right Dragon Stance, you execute a right upper cut with the Poisoned Hand (Tu Shou) to your opponent's chin.

3. Now with your left arm, lock your imaginary opponent's arm by making a big circling movement upward, then outward to your

left, then downward and under his arm, till your left hand can grip his arm from underneath, and his hand and wrist are locked under your left armpit.

4. This is now followed up with a right hand sword strike to your opponent's left side temple.

5. This is the same as No. 5 in the First Set.

6. This is the same as No. 6 in the First Set.

7. This is the same as No. 7 in the First Set.

8. This is the same as No. 8 in the First Set.

The other half of this set, Nos. 9 to 16 are exactly the same as the above but, as in the previous sets, all the arm, hand and leg movements are reversed.

Practise these sets very thoroughly, and slowly at first, until you know the sequences instinctively. Once you know them properly, and can execute each technique perfectly, start thinking of building up your speeds when performing Nos. 2, 3, 4 and Nos. 10, 11, 12 of each set.

If you get into a habit of doing them in a jerky fashion, you will never achieve the grace, fluency and speed that is absolutely necessary. So remember, you must attain the flowing, rhythmic style from one movement to another, which is symbolic of our kind of kung fu. Once you have attained this, speed will come with the flow of movement. Your ultimate goal is to strike those sequences of three blows, one after the other, with the shoulders swinging forward and back to attain maximum momentum, within a period of two seconds.

Chapter 14

Wrist Locks

You will notice that throughout this book all the combat situations that we have dealt with have relied upon your opponent being kept at a distance. This is ideal under certain situations and circumstances, because you have room to move around, see what you are doing, assess the situation, and give yourself time to act accordingly.

When you have gained sufficient experience to dictate the terms of a fight, after you have dealt with any unavoidable skirmishes, you will be able to break away to any position that you wish, from where you will be in a position to manoeuvre freely, and counter attack at your own leisure.

In order to do this, you must be equally skilled at close fighting and capable of turning an attack to your own advantage, so that you can either win at close range, or get away unscathed to a position where you will be out of your opponent's range, yet within range of your own strikes.

However, what if your opponent suddenly and unexpectedly gets hold of your wrists or any part of your body? You could find yourself helpless and open to further attack, because unless you are physically much stronger than him, you won't be able to break free by struggling. In any case the moment you use physical force you are not adhering to the basic principles of Feng Shou.

The success of wrist control, and of arm control, which will be dealt with in Chapter 16, depends not on physical strength at all. It depends on the way you take control and maintain it, and where, with what and how you manipulate it. Should there be any force used at all, let it be your opponent's, and not yours.

A really effective lock controls both the elbow and the wrist joints. If someone is holding one or both of your wrists you may think that he has an advantage over you, but this attitude will immediately put you in a secondary position. You must not think this way, for the mere fact that he holds you does not necessarily mean that he controls you, and control is the absolute essence of any technique: without it you are lost.

Everything will depend on your ability to control him as soon as he gets a hold, then manoeuvre him into a situation whereby you can break or get out of his grip. You must then act quickly to put a hold, a grip or counter-attack of any kind against him as it pleases you.

With what you already know, you can easily break away from a wrist hold or lock, by the simple application of a kick properly executed to one of the many available vulnerable targets, and this would, no doubt, quickly finish your attacker there and then, and within a short space of time. However, Feng Shou kung fu is not, and has never been, an aggressive art — it does not teach or encourage aggression of any kind — so it is not always necessary to be violent, especially as the range of techniques is so wide, that you can always cover every contingency.

Remember this important fact: every time you are called upon to defend yourself, whether this has to be done mentally, verbally, or even physically, you are the judge and the jury and you have to come to a verdict at a split second's notice. You will never have much time in an affray so your decisions have to be made spontaneously. You must know as many alternative forms of defence, counter-attacks, and evasions as possible, and this will give you an all round means of self-defence. This in turn helps to create more confidence within yourself.

Generally speaking, if both of your wrists are held, all you have to do to free yourself is to turn your wrists in a rotary motion, either inward which is towards the centre line of your body, or outward from the body. This has the tendency to twist your opponent's arms, making it impossible for him to hold on to your wrists. Try it and you will be surprised how easy it is to accomplish.

The following moves are rather more complicated so don't rush into them or you could lose yourself completely. Read the text carefully, taking each move at a time, refer to the illustrations and then go slowly through each move with your partner. If you take it slowly you will find that you will learn more quickly in the long run.

1. You will always come across the odd person who in friendliness puts out his hand for a handshake and then, to show you how strong he is, or as a deliberate attempt to hurt you, he squeezes your hand and fingers very hard, and even though he knows that you are in pain, he wont let go. So turn his hand so that the back of his hand faces the floor, then start to lift your hand. With your other hand grip the underside of his wrist and let that hand continue the lift upwards. Your right hand, which was handshaking, is suddenly moved downwards pressing inwards, which will almost take his own hand under his wrist. At this point, due to the pressure and pain he feels on his wrist, you will find that your opponent will start to rise into the air till eventually he is standing on tiptoes. You now have him in a reverse wrist lock and it is very painful.

By moving his hand right or left, you can topple him forward or take him back, and if the technique is executed quickly, he will have no chance at all to use his free hand against you.

2. If your opponent grips your right wrist with his right hand, swing your right arm across to your left, then circle it up and over the top of his right wrist. Lower your hand so that you can place it firmly on his arm. Now with your left hand, lock the fingers of his right hand to your arm, by clamping down on them. Then lower your right hand and forearm downwards towards the floor, pressing down on his right wrist as you do so. In this way you will have trapped him in a simple wrist lock, which will easily

take him down to his knees. Don't apply the pressure in a jerky fashion, rather use a steady and continual thrust.

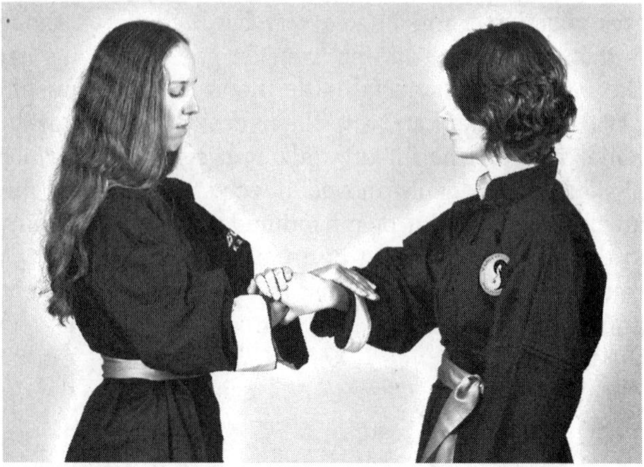

3. Let us try another one from the same situation, whereby your opponent grabs your right wrist with his right hand. This time, circle your right arm across to your left and then upwards as you did before, but when you come down on top of his wrist, instead of just laying on it, actually grip it with your right hand. Again, lock his hand to your own wrist by pressing on the back of his hand with your left hand. Now twist your right hand clockwise to your right, as you push your arm down towards the floor.

If your partner falls towards the floor, you can step backwards as you apply this technique, which will make it even more hazardous for him, and more difficult for him to strike you with his left hand.

4. Here is another way to tackle the same predicament when an opponent grabs your right wrist with his right hand. Swing your right arm to the left, as before, and then take it up and over to your right in a big circle, so that you can get hold of his wrist with your right hand. Now continue that big circle downwards, then back out towards your left, and then again upwards. As you make this last circle, make a strong twist with your right hand, and you will find that your opponent will turn his back towards you, not willingly of course, but he will have no other option, for if he tried to fight against your grip he could break his own arm.

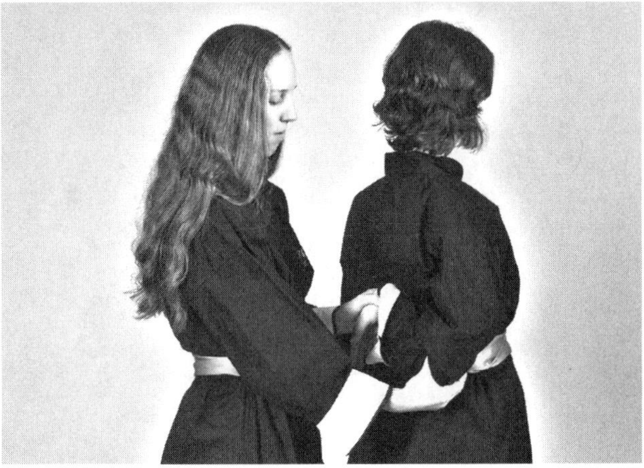

Now place your other hand on the back of his right hand, and gently apply a wrist lock by pressing firmly so that his palm moves towards his own arm. At this point, release your grip on his wrist with your right hand and transfer your hold to a point just above his right elbow. You can then exert enormous pressure very gently by pressing to your left with your right hand, and pressing towards your right with your left hand. His wrist will be under the stress of the two antagonistic squeezing angles. You can then march him off at your leisure.

5. This particular technique can be applied either with one hand or both hands; it depends mainly on how big your hand is, or how strong your grip might be. If you are a woman then you may find that you will have to use both hands against a very strong man. Once more, from a right wrist grip you swing or circle your right arm in an anti-clockwise motion until your arm is above your opponent's arm. At this point, place your left hand on his hand with your thumb resting on the back of his hand and your fingers gripping round his thumb. Swing your right hand inwards towards yourself, and your right arm will break free of his grip. If you press very firmly down with your thumb then you can take him down to the floor with a wrist lock. However, if you cannot get enough

pressure on your one hand, then utilize your right hand as well, by gripping alongside your left hand, and both thumbs can then press together. Remember that this stuff is dynamite, so make your pressure firm but ease it on gently with your partner; don't jerk the pressure when you apply the lock.

6. This time, let your partner grip your right wrist with his left hand, and as you feel his grip, start to rotate your right arm to your right, then upwards. Go over the top of his wrist, and as you are doing this turn your right hand so that by the time you start to come down on top of his arm, your little finger edge of your palm will rest on his wrist. At the same time, lock his fingers to your arm by pressing your left hand down on the back of his hand. Now with your right hand press it firmly and directly downwards towards the floor, keeping the pressure constant on the back of his wrist.

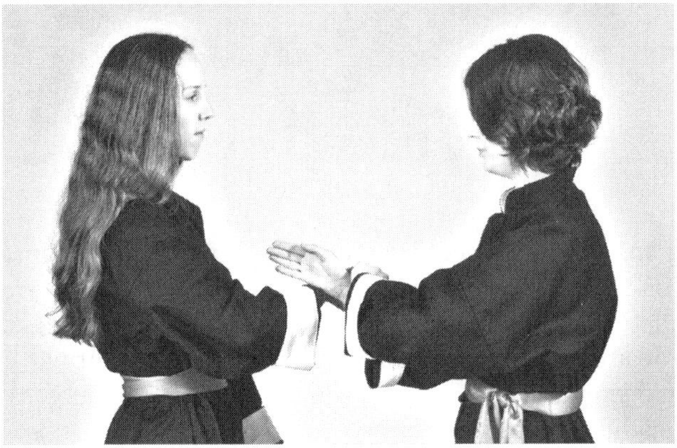

7. Once again your partner grips your right wrist with his left hand, now bring up your right hand and grip his wrist by coming up from underneath — between your first finger and thumb — and at the same time lock his hand on to your arm by placing your left hand on the back of his hand. Now bend his arm back toward himself, twist his wrist inwards with your left hand — that is to say, away from yourself. At the same time also turn his wrist with your right hand, and lower both of your hands straight downwards. This lowering action should be slow, because this wrist twist is extremely painful: be very careful how you apply this lock, and do it slowly until you get the feel of the technique.

Wrist Lock No. 7

8. If an opponent should come up to you from behind and grab both of your wrists, immediately circle both arms forward and around to the front of your body until your right hand can go underneath your left hand. Now grip hold of his right hand from his little finger side with your left hand, and as you turn your body slightly to your left, bring his right arm over your head and out to your left side by a swinging action with your left arm. Twist his wrist and hand outward from yourself, but inwards towards him, and turn your body even more to your left, and he will be drawn backwards very quickly.

You can keep him moving backwards just by the turn of your body, but be very careful, for this is another very powerful wrist twist, and as most of his own body weight is hanging on his arm, through your twisting action, then it can be very painful. You will

notice while doing this technique that you will be able to get rid of his left hand hold without any trouble whatsoever, but by keeping it under your control you succeed in keeping his free hand away from you all the time, so there is no way he can hit back.

9. Another way of overcoming an opponent who takes hold of both of your wrists from behind is a simple progression of No. 8. Once again you draw and circle your arms round your own body until they come to the front of your stomach, and again take his right hand in your left hand grip, slightly turn your shoulders to the left, and swing his arm over the top of your head. Turn your whole body to the left and, at the same time, twist his wrist inwards towards him. Having moved him into this position, now

put your right hand on to his right elbow, and gently lower the elbow down on to your own left arm. Meanwhile, your left hand still keeps up its twisting action, and this provides you with a lot of leverage, which will eventually force him down to the floor. Again be very careful, for the weight of his body is now fully on his right arm and especially on his right wrist. Practise this slowly to get the true feel of it.

Practise these movements with a partner or friend, and to begin with have him act as your opponent, and after you have practised a certain technique, reverse the roles and you be the attacker. This way, both of you will learn what it feels like to apply these locks, and what excruciating pain you feel when you are on the receiving end.

Finally, taking it in turns again, have your friend surprise you at any time by grabbing you suddenly with any one of the different types of offensive actions outlined in this chapter. You will then learn to react instantly with the correct defence and the equivalent counter-attack.

Don't be surprised that in your hurry to get out of his grip, you might react too fast and make a few mistakes, but before long you will find that you will apply the right technique to suit the situation. After a while it will become second nature to you to do the right thing at the correct time. Persevere, and in time each technique and movement will flow into one smooth, continuous action.

Chapter 15

Arm Locks

Whatever the circumstances the first thing a Feng Shou expert will try to do is to gain control of a situation, no matter what type it might be, whether verbally, mentally or physically.

He can do this in several different ways, through a ward-off that puts his opponent in a disadvantageous position, or by using his pure evasion techniques until the opportunity presents itself for a safe strike, or, in particularly close-up conditions or situations, through arm control, or wrist or arm locks.

In the latter, not only can you take control of your assailant's arms when he grips you, but even if he attempts to strike at you, you can ward off his blow in a way that will create an opening so that you take hold of his arm. From then on there are many techniques that can be utilized to suit the situation of yourself, your opponent, and the environment.

In Feng Shou, however, strength does not come into it, because some ninety per cent is through the skilful use of your arms, and the other ten per cent is through the utilization of your legs and body. The true skill within the art is being able to recognize, identify and feel the weaknesses in your opponent's attack, technique, stance, and balance, and within a split second being able to exploit them to the full. Then, even if several people should hold each of your wrists, you can overcome them all, simply by moving against their weaknesses.

If you had, for instance, two people gripping both your wrists, one on either side, then you could struggle and strain against their physical strength, with no avail, and without the remotest chance of breaking free or of getting away. Yet if you took a pace or two backwards, circled both arms round to your own front, and started to walk forward, you could not only keep them in front of you, but they too would have to walk in front of you. You would simply be exploiting their weak points, and you could do this without the slightest use of physical strength, without struggling, and without any strain at all. Even a young girl could do the same thing if she had a man gripping each arm. It is even easier when you have two men gripping each of your arms, because the four of them would make a tight bunch and would get in each other's way, and they would certainly trip over each other's feet.

Through arm locks you can bend your opponent into positions of submission, raise him to great heights and even place him in such a situation that he would be completely inactive. There are hundreds of arm locks and many of them cause no lasting harm if they are executed properly. It is very rare that you should ever need to cause any real harm, so arm locks can be the perfect way of defeating or subduing an opponent, without resorting to more violent action.

Surprisingly, the elbow controls the body, so the use of an arm lock, which in itself controls the elbow joint, must also indirectly influence the body movement, so this must always be your main target. If applied expertly then arm locks require very little force, but speed and skilful application is absolutely essential, and this can only come through constant practice and experience.

Although when you start to practise you will need to take your time until you get the feel of what you are attempting to do, but in actual combat none of the sequences should take more than a second or two from start to finish. Of course, one of the distinguishing factors of the Feng Shou expert is his speed, in every field of his art, which is based upon the harmony of his hands, arms, body, feet, balance, technique, energy, mental training, and evasion movements all synchronized into one flowing movement. The end result therefore shows that the more flowing the movements, the quicker the application and the submission will be.

In Feng Shou we make the best possible use of the entire body's capabilities. This means never using any excess effort, which is why we disprove of and discourage the use of effort, and stress that all things must be fulfilled with the absolute minimum of physical strength, and the greater use of Inner Power (Ch'i). As a matter of fact, the use of physical power has the tendency to slow down the movement of the body, for it creates and causes tension, which tends to contract and reduce the natural power and movement of the individual.

The movement that you will be looking for is very easy to acquire; if you follow the sequences and examples that are outlined in this book, then the correct body flow will come to you quite naturally. However, to master it entirely, then your balance, co-ordination and timing must be perfect. In addition, you will need to be relaxed, confident and self-assured, and give each training session your full attention.

The arm locks that follow not only demand these qualities but, with constant practice, they will also help you to develop your inner self. We have said this before but we must stress this again; practise everything slowly at first, don't try and rush any of the techniques, until you feel confident enough to increase your speed in slow degrees.

Later on, when you do acquire the necessary speeds of mental adaption, physical co-ordination, and intuitive reaction, and when you obtain the complete feel of every movement with each technique, then you will be amazed at the simplicity of handling and controlling your opponent under every conceivable condition and from any form of attack. It all lies within your own capabilities, but don't try and rush into it.

One thing you must remember is that a blow can travel at very high speeds: you must not expect to be able to catch it during its flight for it could be travelling at anything up to sixty miles an hour. You will only be able to grasp your attacker's arm either before the blow starts (and only Feng Shou experts are taught to do this for it takes a lot of training experience to match the split second timing that is involved), or by warding off the blow or evading it, and after it has travelled its full course, just before your opponent starts to pull his blow back, it will stop for a fraction of a second and that is the time to make your move to either grip his wrist or to take the arm under control to apply an arm lock.

For many of the following techniques alternatives are given, and it is essential for you to know them. You may have a favourite move or a preference for dealing with a particular situation with a special sequence, but if your opponent should execute an attacking action or an arm lock that you are not familiar with, if you have restricted yourself to only a few techniques there could be difficulties, although not necessarily insurmountable problems.

To make your task a little easier, we have included some of the common ways of extricating yourself from a number of normal holds, and you should therefore be able to turn them into your advantage, once you have acquired the necessary skills.

1. When an opponent tries to strangle you from the front with both hands don't, whatever you do, try and grab his wrists and endeavour to pull his arms away as this will have the tendency of tightening his grip on your throat.

With this technique you can turn either way, but as an example let us rotate to the left. Swing your right arm upwards in a big circle, over the top of his arms and then down towards your right side. You will find that you have not only broken his grip from your throat, but you have also locked both of his arms under your armpit. You can then march him off quite effortlessly. Instead of turning to the left, try it again by swinging to the right and using your left arm. Whilst you are swinging your arm over, make sure that your body also keeps turning away.

2. Another alternative release from a two-handed strangle hold on your throat is a very simple technique — so simple that at first it seems ludicrous, yet it really works: try it! With both of your open hands press firmly against the outside of your opponent's wrists, pressing both hands inwards towards one another. As you do this, step back about twelve inches with both feet and you will find that his hands will slide easily off your neck. Now bring one of your elbows over the top of his arms, lock them under your armpit, keeping your grip on his wrists, and you will have him in another double arm lock.

3. Another technique from a two-handed grip on your neck, is to bend your head and your shoulders straight forward and downwards very deeply, then circle the upper part of your body to either the right or to the left. Return to the upright position, and you will find that both of his arms are lying on your shoulder. Turn towards his arms and swing your nearest arm over the top of both of his. Now catch his wrists with your other hand, bear your shoulder weight down on his upper arms, and slowly raise his wrists upwards towards the ceiling. This will put him in a very strong arm lock, and his knees will buckle with the force of the technique.

Release No. 3, Move 1

Release No. 3, Move 2

4. The fourth alternative release from a double hand strangle-hold on your throat is to place either the flat of your hand against the centre of his chest or, if your arm is shorter than his, place the front of your fist in the same position. Then raise your other arm between both of his arms, swing it through and outwards, over the top of the nearest arm to it, and then under that arm so that it completely entwines it. Use the hand of the entwining arm to take over the position of the other hand, resting on his chest. Now stiffen your entwining arm so that it becomes almost straight, and at the same time push with that hand firmly on his chest. Now turn your free shoulder back away from your opponent, and this finalizes the locking in of your opponent into

Release No. 4, Move 1

Release No. 4, Move 2

an arm lock. It is a very subtle movement but, like all techniques in the soft arts of China, it has great potential.

5. To deal with a strangle-hold that is applied from behind with both hands, first of all swing your right leg in front of your left, so that it rests about eighteen inches beyond. At the same time, deeply dip your body down and turn your head and shoulders to the left, whilst you pivot on your left foot. This will not only bring your body and your head and shoulders down and under both of his arms, but if you continue the pivoting movement on your left foot, the grip around your throat will be broken. Turn towards his arms as you stand up, and bring your left arm over the top of his

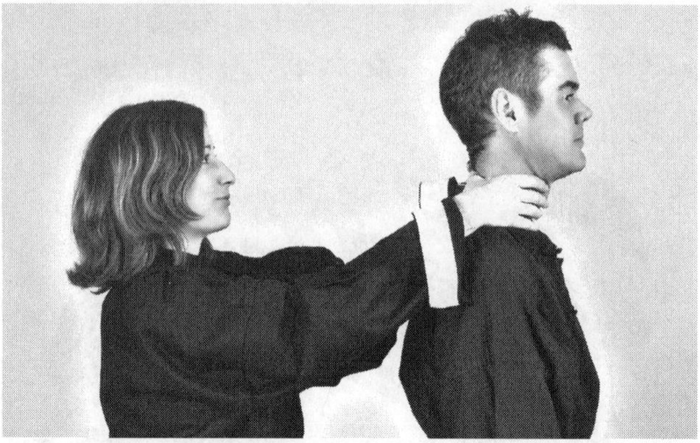

Release No. 5, Strangle Hold

Release No. 5, Move 1

Release No. 5, Move 2

whilst your right hand catches his wrists. Bear down with your body on his upper arms, raise his wrists slightly, and you will be able to keep him there as long as you maintain the pressure on his upper arms.

6. If your opponent puts you in an arm strangle-hold from the rear, with his right arm round your neck and the other hand holding his own wrist, repeat the same action as before, pivoting on the left foot, but, as you bend your body down, turn your head towards his hands, so that your chin fits into the gap between his wrists and his body.

Make sure that you don't stand upright too soon, though, because your head must be completely clear of his arms. Now put your left hand on his hip and push it away from you, thereby making the gap bigger. Slip your right arm in-between your opponent's two arms and bring it to your left and upwards until it makes contact with his right upper arm. Now firmly press down with your right hand, and you have him in a bent arm lock. To guarantee that he cannot escape, catch his right wrist with your left hand, and he is now powerless, and you can march him off at your will, or put him straight down to the floor.

7. A similar position could arise where an opponent tries to strangle you from behind, with his right arm round your neck, but this time he grips your left wrist with his left hand. First, put your right hand on to his right wrist and hold it firmly to your own body. Turn the same way as you did in the previous move,

not forgetting to turn your head so that your chin lies in the gap between his wrist and his body, and once your head is completely clear of his arm, start to lift his right wrist upwards towards his shoulder. As he starts to bend forward because of the pain and leverage, bring your left hand on to his right wrist. When you have got hold of it, let go with your right hand and place it just above his right elbow, and you have him in a bent arm lock.

8. If you happen to face your opponent and he suddenly grips your right wrist with his right hand, circle your right arm out to your left, then up and over his right wrist until you are able to grip it with your right hand. Then bring it down to a position near to your right hip. Put your left hand on his elbow and gently apply a downward pressure, but still keep the wrist well up, and your opponent will fall to the floor. When he puts out his left hand to save himself from falling onto his face, step back with your right foot, followed immediately by your left, drawing him with you as you go. He has to fall onto his chest as his left hand cannot support his body and you can completely trap him by applying a straight arm lock.

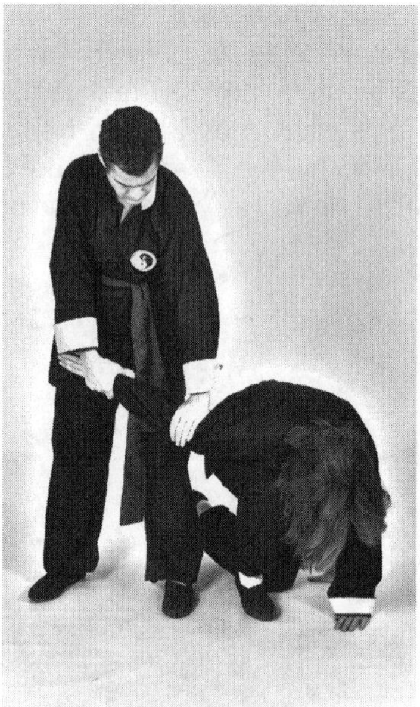

9. If an opponent takes both of your wrists from the front, one in each hand, bring your hands inward towards one another, then swing them upwards and then outwards until you are over the top of his wrists. Then you are in a position to grasp both of his wrists. When you have got a good grip on them, start to twist them outwards, both going in opposite directions, right hand twisting to the right, left hand twisting to the left, and when they have been twisted to at least 180° the palms of your hands should be facing upwards towards the ceiling. Now lever your own hands so that you press on the top of his wrists with the heels of your palms, and raise the finger edge of your hand. This added action should straighten his arms, creating a straight arm lock on both arms, and if you lean slightly backwards at the same time you will have added leverage.

Chapter 16

Arm Control

Correct Arm Control (Pei Yueshu) exploits the stability of your opponent's stance and the full weaknesses of body balance, some of which are already familiar to you through your practice of the Adhering Hand techniques. With the 'feel' of the technique, and the skill that you acquire from its continuous practice, you will be able to move your opponent anywhere at will.

This control of your opponent's balance and stance is gained through the use of your arms, and the utilization of his arms, body and legs, to your own full advantage. For instance, if he should attempt to strike you, you would ward off his blow and therefore get the chance of taking hold of his arm, and then control can seriously begin.

Similarly, if he holds you, then his arms are temporarily static, so you can easily turn this situation to your own advantage by taking control of his arms. This in turn will give you the opportunity of moving his shoulders, body or legs as you wish, in any direction.

In our arts, 'arm control' means that your opponent must be able to walk or move on his feet, but under your full control at all times. If you should lock him down on the floor, then this is not arm control, because he must be able to move around, but under your strict control. There are two methods of obtaining control: the first is a 'loose control' where you can make your opponent's balance move a few inches or as much as two or three feet off its line of movement, and the force and skill of your execution will enable you to put him in any desired position without actually gripping him at all. The second, which is known as 'positive control', means that you can actually grip him with your hand, arm, arm pit, body or legs and move him into any position or in any direction that you have already chosen.

Let us try both methods to get the feel of this Arm Control technique, and, by the way, it means the use of your own arm and not necessarily your opponent's arm. Let him grip your right wrist with his right hand, now circle your arm first out to your left, then upwards and back to your right so that you are over the top of his wrist, and you now grip it with your right hand. Now start to turn your body to your right, and as you do so draw your opponent forward with your right hand so that he has to move his feet to maintain his balance. As soon as he begins to move, keep drawing with your right hand, whilst turning on the spot you are standing on. You will find that you will be able to keep him moving continuously in a circle around you, with very little effort on your part. This is an example of positive control: keeping your opponent under your strict control through the medium of your grip. Its contact enables you to control his movements and the extent of his balance, so that you can dictate the speed and direction of his enforced weakness.

Loose control can be executed from a similar technique. As you swing your hand over the top of his wrist, press it down smartly towards the floor; at the same time, slide your hand down his arm with as long a hand sweep that you can possibly manage. You will find that he has a tendency to tip his body weight forward, and may even have to move his feet to retain his balance, and this is executed without even gripping his arm or wrist. You can easily change the direction that you wish him to go, by sweeping his arm directly sideways, upwards, or downwards just by varying the degree of circle of your own arm, and the

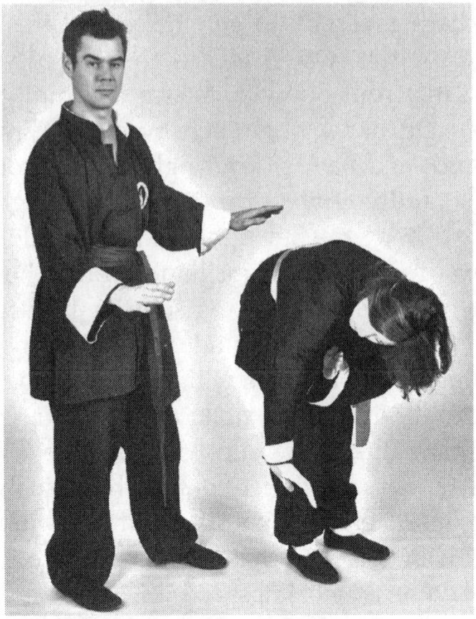

position of contact on his arm where your hand can rest to start your press, push or lift.

In Feng Shou kung fu, strength is not required, because some ninety per cent of the power used is through the skilful use of internal energy (Ch'i), and the other ten per cent is through the utilization of body and leg movements. The real skill is in identifying the weaknesses that always exist in your opponent's stance and balance, and then, having found one, to fully exploit it in the short space of time available. When you are being attacked, time is the one thing that is extremely scarce, so speed is of the utmost importance, especially if you want to ensure that your opponent does not have the opportunity to escape or counter-attack.

One of the distinguishing factors of a Feng Shou expert is his speed which is based upon beautiful synchronized movements, acquired through hard work over a long period of time. The essence, of course, is the flowing movement that is necessary within the application of any technique and the greater the flow, the faster the speed.

Should several people hold you by each wrist, therefore, you can overcome them not by moving against their points of strength, but by finding their weaknesses and then moving into them or taking advantage of the areas that are presented to you. For example, if you had four opponents gripping your wrists, two on either side, you could struggle and strain without making the slightest impression against your attackers, and would not stand the slightest chance of getting away. However, if you took a couple of paces backward, drawing your arms round to the front of your body, then all you have to do is to keep them in front of yourself, and walk forward against their weak points.

They will be going backwards, and their balance will be very unstable. With the four of them in a tight bunch, they will trip over each other's feet in a very short space of time and you can increase their predicament by altering the directions of their movement by pulling a little stronger on one hand thus drawing them even closer together.

These are only a few examples of arm control, loose and positive, and you can adapt them to any form of attack. In loose control not only can you affect the arm, but if your ward-off is strong enough you can lay the other hand on your opponent's arm, shoulder, body, or hips and push him away strongly in any direction that you choose, or you can make it a positive control by gripping any part of his body.

Chapter 17

Press Downs

To 'press down' (An Chu) in our art means that by applying a technique, you take, or make your opponent go down on to the floor, either on his back or his front, and pin him there for a minimum period of five seconds. He must remain completely under your control not only as he is being forced down, but also during the period that you wish to keep him on the floor.

Now this seems simple enough, but when a person attacks you it is difficult enough to control his aggressive action, by warding off his blow. You must then affect a positive arm control action, and then, ensuring that your control is good enough, take him to the floor, completely under your supervision. This is a lot of work in a very little time, and meanwhile he will still be trying to get at you somehow — he won't be giving up that easily. How do we go about it?

Let us start with a few examples using some of the techniques that have been outlined in previous chapters, and which you have already practised and with which you have acquired a certain degree of skill.

Execute arm-lock No. 1 against a strangle hold by your partner, and after locking both his arms under your armpit, grip his wrists with both of your hands so that there is no chance of him getting free. Now as you turn your body away put your body weight on to his arms, and sit down on the floor. Practise this very slowly at first, for remember that you have both of his arms tied up, and therefore when you sit down, your weight will force his shoulders downward, and he has no hands or arms free to save himself. If you are too forceful or do it too quickly in practise, he could easily crash down on to his shoulder and break it, for not only has he got his own weight moving downwards but your weight as well. Once his legs start to give way under this pressure you will find that at a certain point they will suddenly collapse. Once you have successfully taken him to the floor, you can peg him there by resting your body weight on to his chest, still locking his arms under your armpit and maintaining your grip on his wrists.

You can then practise the same press-down with arm locks No. 2 and No. 3, but with arm lock No. 4 you can execute a press-down by pressing with your hand on his chest, leaning slightly backwards and lifting up his elbow with your entwining arm. At the same time, so that he cannot pick up his balance, place one of your feet behind the heel of the leg that is nearest to you. As he starts to stagger backwards, lean backwards more strongly yourself, and he will have to fall to the floor. Again, let us repeat our caution to practise *slowly* so that no accidents will happen to your partner. Once you have him on his back on the floor, get on to your knees and you can hold him indefinitely there with your arm lock.

You can also apply your press-downs when you have got your opponent in any of the various forms of wrist locks or other arm locks, and it is well worthwhile to try to finish the movement and technique all the way down to the floor. You will also be able to march your opponent off under the stress of a lock.

There are other ways of applying press-downs without the application of wrist or arm locks, and this is mainly through the use of spot pressing on various points of the body. However, this will need a lot of practising for you have to make contact with a specific point first time and then pressure must be instantaneous, because your opponent is not going to stand still while you fiddle around, trying to find the right spot.

1. Let us say that your opponent throws a blow at your chin, which you ward off to the outside of his arm. Now execute a loose control by pushing his arm strongly away from yourself. This should make him turn his shoulders so that he may be partly turned away or if your movement has been proficient he may even have turned his back to you. Let us say he has done the latter. Now place both hands on his shoulders, and with your middle finger press straight down into the hollow of the collar bone. If you find the pressure point correctly, and the pressure applied is strong enough, you will see his knees immediately buckling and you will be able to sit him down on his backside without any more trouble, holding him there for as long as you

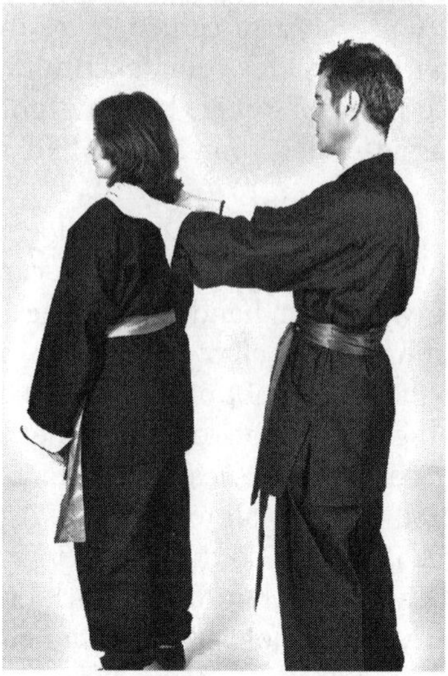

like. Because he will still want to get away from the pressure of your fingers, you will find that he tries to move backwards on to his back. To stop this movement, which will weaken your pressure, put one of your legs into the middle of his back as soon as he sits down: this will stop him falling any further backwards. It will also ensure that he is literally rooted to one spot by the pressure of two fingers.

2. Having warded off another blow at your chin and executed a strong loose control on your opponent's arm so that he once more turns his back towards you, then place your thumbs just above the hip bone, on either side of his body. Now press firmly inwards, just as if both thumbs were moving towards each other. Now change direction and press directly downward. If he is ticklish he will immediately collapse, but if he is not then you will again see his knees bending until they reach a point when he just collapses, and sits down on the floor. You can hold him there with that pressure, and help to reinforce this press-down by putting your knee into the middle of his back, or, if you wish, you can roll him over onto his stomach so that he is face down, and place your knee into his back to pin him firmly on the ground.

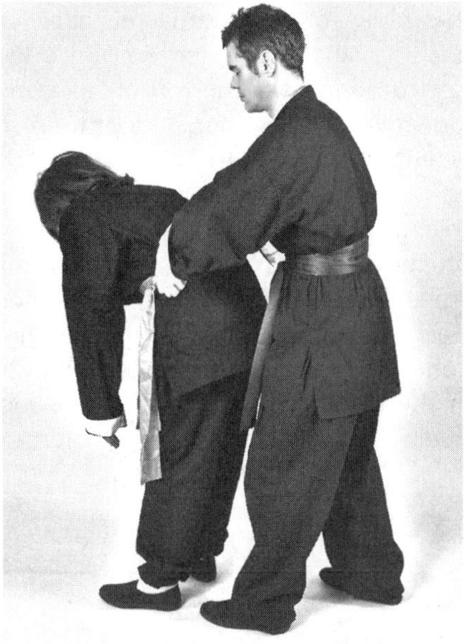

Press Down No. 2, Move 1

Press Down No. 2, Move 2

3. As another blow comes towards your face, ward off to the outside of your assailant's arm then execute a loose control by taking your arm up and over the top of his arm. At this point press firmly downwards with your own arm so that your loose control is directed downwards towards the floor. You will find that all the tension in his arm has disappeared and that both knees have started to bend slightly.

Now press on the inside of his thigh, approximately half-way between his knee and his groin, with your middle finger or with the Tiger's Head (Laohu T'ou). He will fall directly sideways towards you, and if you retain that pressure you can pin him to the floor with the same pressure. Don't press too hard at first, until you get the true feel of it, because it is extremely painful.

4. Your partner aims another blow at your face, and after warding off his attacking arm, grip his wrist, and put him immediately into a straight arm lock by placing your other hand on his elbow and applying leverage on the arm. Now, through your lock, take him all the way down to the floor, so that he is forced to lie flat on his stomach. To keep him there without strain, place your middle finger, or your Tiger's Head, into his back midway between his shoulder-blade and his spine, and press firmly downward. Don't apply too much pressure at first, and you will soon acquire the feel of how much to apply to keep him trapped to the floor.

5. Once more go through exactly the same procedure as in No. 4 by taking your partner down to the floor with your straight arm lock, but this time place a foot on his upper arm, and then gently bend his arm so that his forearm lies across your shin. You have now fully trapped him to the floor and he will be unable to rise. If you want to apply leverage to your lock, very slowly move your leg forward by bending your knee. Be very careful: do not use hard pressures, don't jerk any movement and, for goodness sake, take it very easily when applying the final leverage — this lock is dynamic. You have now fulfilled your aim by pressing him down to the floor and trapping him there.

These are just a few of the many techniques that can be used to keep your opponent on the floor, and under your constant control. Make use at first of all the wrist and arm locks that you know, and learn to apply them so that, under your controlled pressure and the power of your technique, your partner will have no option but to sink down to the floor. Then you can keep him there with very little effort on your part.

Chapter 18

Break-Outs

Feng Shou is such a gentle art that violent and aggressive actions are not necessary in the various situations that could arise, though we hope they never will. Providing you have learnt to recognize the weaknesses in your opponent's stances, balance, movement and technique, from the experience you have gained in your practice, then you will always have the advantage when applying your own counter-technique. Of course, you must also have built up your speed in thought, observation, and movement so that you can take full advantage of any opportunity that may present itself. If you should react a little slowly in your execution of a possible counter then you could easily miss the chance which had presented itself to you, and in a tense situation this is something that you can ill afford to do.

If someone should happen to grip you, then they will not only hold you really tightly but they will be using as much strength as possible in their endeavour to keep your under control, and to stop you fighting your way out. But as soon as your opponent grips you, you will give him his first surprise: you won't try and fight out, neither will you struggle. This will upset his plans for he will automatically expect you to do both, and this is your first advantage.

Your second advantage will be the control that you have over your attacker, even though he is holding you. The third advantage that you have is the technique that you apply after you have broken out of his grasp. So let us start on your break-outs from a variety of grips and holds.

1. Your partner stands directly in front of you and grips your right wrist with his right hand. To break out of his grip is very easy indeed. All you need to do is to circle your right hand out to

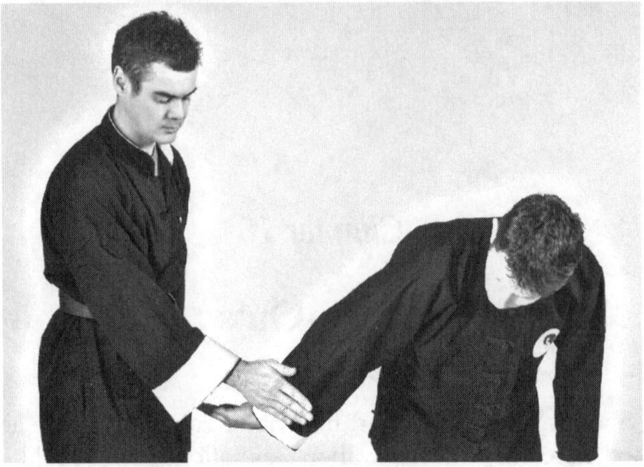

Break Out No. 1, Move 1

Break Out No. 1, Move 2

your right, and as you do so rotate your wrist so that your right palm faces upwards. Now continue to circle your hand upwards and then to your left, and keep rotating your wrist so that the palm of your hand faces downwards as your right wrist moves over the top of your opponent's hand. If you continue moving your hand and wrist to your left you will find that you will slip quite easily out of his grip.

2. Now let your partner grip your right wrist with both of his hands as he stands in front of you, and execute the same circling action as you have just done in break-out No. 1, but this time make your rotary action a little bigger, for you have to move your

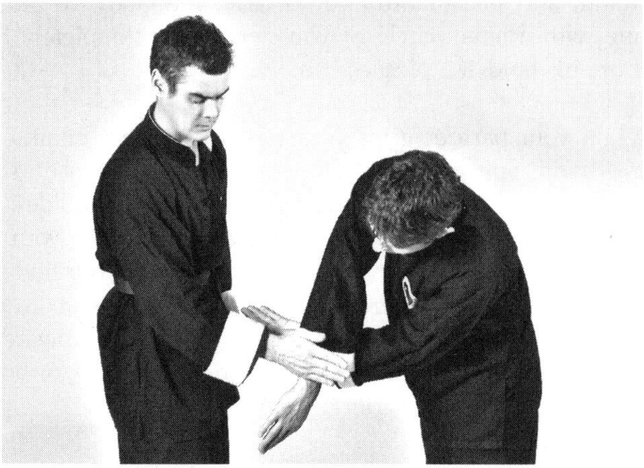

hand and wrist round both of his arms. Having got your hand above his arms you continue going to your left, but once you have gone beyond his arms then circle your hand and wrist downward. This will bring your hand back almost to the point that it originally started from when he first gripped your wrist.

3. Get your partner to grip your right wrist with his right hand again. This time start circling your hand and wrist to your left, and make a complete circle round his wrist. You will find that you will break away from his grip quite easily.

4. Now let your partner grip your right wrist with both of his hands, and execute the same circling action that you did in No. 3. Ensure this time that you make a slightly bigger circle, because of the two arms that are holding you.

5. Practise the same circling action when he grips your right wrist with his left hand, and don't forget to get the feel of circling both ways for your break-outs.

6. Get your partner to come up to you from behind and grip your right wrist with his right hand. Spin your body to your right, by pivoting on your right leg and swinging your left leg round in a big arc, until you face your partner. Simultaneously, swing your right arm in a big circle to the left, then upward, and then to the right. At this point your right hand should be over the top of your partner's wrist. You can grip his wrist if you want to, with your

right hand, and take control of his arm and body, or you can continue with a small circle of your wrist and completely break away from his hold, if it pleases you.

7. Again your partner grips your right wrist from behind with his right hand. Spin to your left this time and, as you do so, lift your right arm into the air above your right shoulder. Your partner's arm is now above your head. Continue your arm movement by dropping your arm down in front of your body, and his arm will be straight in front of you too. If you want to circle out of his grip just rotate your wrist from left, then upward and out to your right, or you can grip him with either hand, or both at the same time, to maintain control over him.

8. Your partner creeps up behind you and grips you round the neck with his left arm, and then he grips his left hand with his right hand, and locks your neck in his embrace. Then he really starts to squeeze, which doesn't do your windpipe much good. However, it is easy to get out of this hold, without using any violence, so you have no need to worry. All you have to do is step a few inches to the left with your left foot, followed immediately

Break Out No. 8, Neck Lock

Break Out No. 8, Move 1

Break Out No. 8, Move 2

with your right foot, and swing your hips to the left as well, as far as you can. Now step back one pace with your right foot only, turn your body slightly towards your partner and, as you do so, bend forward very deeply and quickly, turning your head to the right. As you bend down place your right hand on his bottom, and push, and you will send your partner flying in front of you and your head will slide free very easily. Keep practising this combination of movements for you can use them in quite a number of different angles and grips, and once you have acquired the skill of being able to break away smoothly and swiftly, you will find that it only takes a few seconds to free yourself of his hold, but you must learn to synchronize all the movements together into one flowing technique.

9. But what happens if he should grip you round the neck in the same fashion, but holds you trapped against his waistline while he squeezes, and keeps you in the bent down position?

Break Out No. 9, Move 1

Break Out No. 9, Move 2

Well, have you ever had a really strong sneeze, and got the feeling that you were going to blow your head off? If you have, you will remember that your head went back as you took in a breath, and then you suddenly had to bend forward as you sneezed into your handkerchief. We are going to emulate this same action. First, stand up quickly taking your head back, and just as quickly suddenly bend down very deeply, turning your head inwards towards your partner, keeping your chin tucked in to yourself. The nearest hand you have to your partner, place on his bottom and push as your body bends down, then watch him fly away, and you are free. Simple, isn't it?

10. Your partner now puts both of his hands round your throat, as he stands in front of you, and tries to strangle you. Of course, just because you have two hands free and both legs free, you might easily think that you can resort to force, and either hit him or kick him, but by doing so there is still no guarantee that he is going to release his grip, and in the short time that you have got, you could still get strangled. Why not try our gentle and non-violent way, and still ensure that you break away cleanly and

effortlessly from this type of attack. All you have to do is place the second finger (the longest finger) of your right hand in the hollow of your partner's neck just below the Adam's Apple, keeping the finger straight and firm. Now press forward and, as you do so, turn your shoulders to the left so that your right shoulder comes forward, and you will find that your partner will only be too pleased to let go of his hold. Be gentle and be careful for it can be very nasty when you are on the receiving end.

These are a few simple ways of breaking away from your opponent's grips and holds, without the slightest use of strength, force, or violence, but by pure and simple technique. They can be done by anyone, weak or strong, tall or short, without the slightest strain or having to match the brute strength of an attacker.

Of course, these are only a few to give you the feel of our break-out techniques, and there are thousands more. They will be passed on to you if you follow our Feng Shou style: write to us to find out where your nearest club or instructor might be.

Practise every technique over and over again, so that eventually every minute movement is synchronized together to make one flowing action. You will be amazed how easy it is, and all techniques are done without using the slightest force or any brute strength whatsoever. This is the deep beauty of Feng Shou: complete self-discipline of oneself, no violence, no strength, and yet a beautiful science of techniques all based on the Taoist principles of the Yin and Yang. Nothing is opposed when harmony can unite everything, and even being attacked does not mean you have to be in opposition; you can overcome through amalgamation and harmony.

Bear this in mind throughout your life, in your work and in your spare time, and you will find that even in the deepest depression there is harmony in a break-out. This way nothing will ever get you down. A depression is Yin and the break-out is Yang, and that is the balance of the two primary forces of the Tao. Understand this, and you understand everything.

Chapter 19

Ankle Control

Ankle Control (Hua Yueshu) is a term that we use in our arts for the control of the whole of your opponent's legs, from the ankle right up to the hips. We are the only style that has this form of control in its curriculum; no other art incorporates such a range of techniques that will not only make kicks miss their intended targets, but make them fly off in a multitude of directions, leaving your attacker not only helpless for fractions of time, but with many parts of his body open and therefore unprotected.

It is impossible to describe the hundreds of techniques involved, and cover every single variation of kick that makes up our art - all we can do is to present some of the simple basic ones that you can practise with a partner and so get the feel of the principles involved.

We are going to start with the control of Foot Flow Pattern No. 1, because if you can control this one pattern you will find that it will also be adaptable to Patterns No. 2 and 3. First of all let us consider the six points of weakness that show up in every single stance, and which are a part of every kick. You must memorize them, and aim to achieve these angles when you practise our Ankle Control techniques.

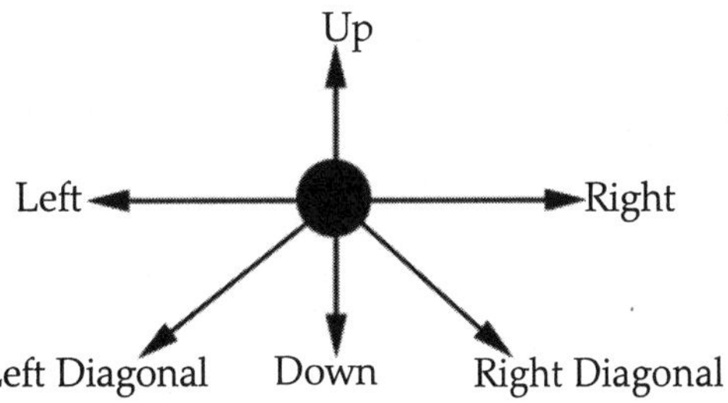

The centre dot represents the lowest balance point of the body, which is the hips, so all the angles emanate from there. We shall be covering five of these directions. The sixth one — up — is too dangerous to practise in these early stages, and only our senior grades and masters learn how to handle it.

Of course, if you happen to get kicked then the fight is more or less over, for you won't be in a position to do much more after that, even if you are still conscious. So before you start practising this particular section you must have fully covered all the other chapters in this book. Failure to do so, like trying to jump before you can walk is certainly asking for trouble. Trying to control something that is moving at about forty miles an hour is no joke, and you have therefore got to have plenty of experience in all forms of ward-offs, all your stances and, more importantly, the evasion exercises. If you don't move your feet and the balance of your body quickly enough, then you've had it. So do not approach this chapter until you have fully mastered everything else in this book. For those who have truly mastered everything else, you are ready to commence practising the techniques here, and you will need a partner who is just as experienced in our art as you.

Start by practising the flowing backward and forward movement of Foot Flow Pattern No. 1, both you and your opponent taking it in turns to swing your right leg into the air. As that foot swings up towards you, you automatically move slightly back so that you are out of range of his kick. It is at this point, as the kick is swinging up in front of your body, that you have got to try to make contact with his ankle with your right hand.

This is not so easy at first, and the best way to practise it is to allow your right hand to flow ahead of your partner's foot on its upward movement and then, as it swings back to the floor, let your hand follow it down as far as you can without bending your body. Don't let your hand touch his leg at all, and certainly don't let his foot or leg strike your hand. Just try and keep your hand a few inches away from his ankle, until you have learnt to judge the speed, the range, the angle, and the height that the foot will reach, and so you can co-ordinate your hand movement to every movement of his leg. Even if you have to practise this a million times it will be worthwhile, for many different techniques will spring from the experience that you gain in this simple procedure. Once you have got the idea with the right hand, try this simple exercise for ranging on with your left hand but still remaining in your right style. Be careful, however, when you are practising this with the opposite hand and leg because you have a tendency to bring the body forwards a little more and therefore, unless you have an excellent eye for your range and the distance involved, you are liable to get kicked. So once again, a word of warning: be careful! Once you have acquired the feel of it on the one side, then change into left style, and practise it with your left hand first, then with the right hand.

1. Let us go back into our right style, and using the right hand. Now, when your partner kicks up in Pattern No. 1, at the height of the kick let your right hand rest lightly on his right ankle. Then, as the foot starts to swing back down, start to press strongly and at the same time let your hand slide from his ankle all the way down the foot till your hands slide off the top of his toes. If you do this correctly and strongly enough on your press-down you will hear his foot pound into the floor, and you may notice that his body has a tendency to jerk forward.

2. Once you have got the feel of doing this correctly with your right hand and right leg, practise the same action still in the right style, with the left hand. Remember to take your partner's foot straight down to the floor, under your control, with a firm press-down and the long slide off from his ankle to the tips of his toes. But don't get careless when you use your left hand in right style for your partner's foot gets dangerously close, so you must

appreciate your degree of distance and range, especially if you happen to be a short person.

3. Again, both of you remain in right style, and this time we want you to use both hands together to control his ankle. This can be executed in two ways: you can either have one hand on top of the other or both hands can be kept side by side. Try both ways till you eventually choose the one that suits your own particular build. Remember, a good press-down and long sliding action should finish the movement off, and make sure that you take your partner's foot straight down to the floor.

4. Now switch to left style, and both of you try this first ankle control with your left hand only. If you are naturally right-handed then you may find your left hand control a little weak, and the timing of your hand not as good as your right, so spend a little longer trying to strengthen this side.

5. Both of you keep in left style and now try this same ankle control with your right hand. Don't forget that you will have to turn your shoulders a little more to get your hand situated correctly on the ankle of your opponent, and that means that your body will be closer to his kick. So keep alert, and practise slowly until you truly get the feel of the whole situation.

6. Still in left style, now learn to utilize both of your hands at the same time. Some of you may find it easier to execute this movement with both hands, and you may obtain better and stronger control over his ankle this way, but watch out for his kick, which will be getting very close.

7. Let us go back into right style, and this time we are going to learn how to control our opponent's leg into the right diagonal position. Start by using the right hand, and the action is similar to the previous ankle control action. Ride ahead of the force of the kick as your partner's kick travels upward and then, as his leg starts to swing down, make contact with his ankle. Now you do not have a lot of time, but as soon as his foot gets to about tummy height, form your right hand fingers into a hook, and strongly pull his leg to your right. Your partner may partly turn his back towards you, or if your movement is strong enough you may even be able to spin his body around 360°. This is a beautiful

technique, with really outstanding results. But don't let us spend too much admiration on one technique when you are beginning to appreciate that the whole of our art is really wonderful.

8. Still keeping in your right stance, this time use your left hand. Ride your hand up with the rise of his foot, but as it starts to drop back to the floor, use the left sun palm and push strongly, and you may get even better results than you did with No. 7.

9. Still executing Pattern No. 1 in right style, now practise using both hands simultaneously. The beauty of taking your opponent's leg into right down diagonal is that he never knows which way he is going to go. In addition to the variation of direction you can use either your left or your right hand — or, better still, you can start the technique with your right hand and finish it off with your left. You can even use both hands together to complete your ankle control, by hooking with your right and pushing with your left. So you have a large variety of techniques at your disposal. Go ahead; use them, and enjoy the enormous scope that this art gives to you.

10., 11., 12. Both you and your partner now change over into left style and you use exactly the same techniques: the right hand hooking, the left hand pushing, and then both hands operating together, with the same objective of taking your partner's leg to the right down diagonal position. There is a great deal of work lying ahead for you, so don't rush yourself, take your time and practise regularly at every opportunity and the results of your labour will prove themselves in time.

13. Once again adopt your right style postures, and we shall now take your partner's leg down into the left diagonal position. Let us start with our right hand which we place on the ankle in our normal ankle control position. As your partner's leg is dropping, turn your hand into a right sun palm and give your opponent's ankle a strong push. You already know the results that you can get from this technique.

14. Still in right style, now let us use the left hand to take our partner's leg down into the left diagonal direction. It is simply done by forming the fingers of the left hand into hooks, and hooking the ankle down to the left just as you previously did with your right hand in No. 7.

15. This time we shall be using both hands, as you are in your right style Foot Pattern No. 1. Remember the left hand will be hooking, and the right will be executing your right sun palm push, so practise diligently and don't forget to adapt to all the techniques so that you can attain perfection.

16., 17., 18. Both you and your partner now switch to left style once more and practise the right sun palm, the left hooks, and the double hand combination. By this time you should be getting very good with your ankle control, but don't give up your training for the ultimate is still a long way off, and only sincere dedication will get you there.

19. Now we are going to execute our ankle control directly to the left, and you will notice from our original drawing of the six directions that it is on a level with the hips of your partner. When you executed the left and right diagonal you may have noticed that your partner's leg dropped fairly quickly after your hand had lost contact with his ankle. To keep the leg in the air for a longer period we not only use the sun palm technique, but we also place the heel of our palm just under the ankle bone of our partner so we are able to keep the leg in the air longer, especially as it gives us a much longer pushing action. So you and your partner get into right style practising Foot Flow Pattern No. 1. Gain your ankle control as his leg rises, and as soon as possible, get your sun palm fitting quickly against his ankle. Now push strongly with your right hand with the heel of the palm slightly under the ankle bone, and try to make it a long pushing movement. Be careful, because you can really upset his balance with this one: be gentle at first until you get the feel of the movement, and know just how far you need to go to get the result that you want.

20. Now change into left posture and try the same technique using the right hand again.

21. Change into right style and this time use your left sun palm and take your partner's leg to the right side direction, and don't forget to fit the heel of your palm just under his ankle.

22. Move again into left style, and still learn to use your left sun palm ankle control to the right direction.

Well! You can appreciate that we were not joking when we said there is a lot of work in our art, and now you can fully understand why. However, even the techniques we have explained here are only scratching the surface but at least they should lay the foundation for your strict control of your partner's leg through the medium of his ankle.

Chapter 20

Inner Power

An old Chinese proverb says that 'The reflection on a pool of water never shows its depth'. In order to prove this, it is necessary for you to get into the water and swim down to the bottom of the pool, for you can never really know anything just by looking or watching. You must go in and see for yourself, or, in the modern idiom, you've got to have a go.

So it is with the Chinese martial arts. One punch might look like any other, but it is what is behind it that really counts. In our style of Feng Shou kung fu, the driving force and the hidden power is Ch'i (internal energy) and this is the most important aspect of our particular art. Its force is dynamic, its utilization fantastic, its benefit to the health of the individual is beyond normal comprehension, and it can be used to heal others.

However, if it is beyond normal comprehension, how do we go about explaining it? It is like trying to teach someone to ride a bicycle. You can tell them how to get on, how to steer, and show them where the brakes are and how to use them. But you cannot explain the very basic fundamental principle: how to maintain the balance so that they can stay on it. Neither can you explain the split-second reaction of when to apply the brakes to stop. Both things can only be learnt through experience, and experience can only come through getting on that bike and having a go.

Certainly you will fall off a few times until you get the feel of control: you will squeeze the brake too hard and nearly disappear over the handlebars, or put on the brake a fraction of a second too late and hit something. But one thing is sure: you will learn through your own practical experience. Some will give up because they find it more difficult than they realized, others will stick at it until they have conquered the principles.

This also applies to the development of inner power. We can

explain to you what it is — we know where it comes from, how to control it, how to cultivate it to make it stronger, we know what it can do, and we know how to use it. But to put it all down in simple terminology, in such a way that you fully grasp the depths of its true meaning, is no easy task.

However, we will do our best, although we can only convey to you the principles by which it works, and give you an impression of its dynamic power. If you wish to go into it more thoroughly, and to acquire the feel of it, and learn to control it, then you must join one of our clubs and practise. In other words, like the cyclist you have to get on the bike and ride it yourself, to get the full understanding and appreciation of its meaning.

Inner Power (Neichung Ch'i) is also known technically as 'intrinsic energy' (T'ien Jan Neng Li), although most people who practise our Taoist arts call it the 'vitality power' (Sheng Ch'i). It is an intangible force which is invisible to the eye: it cannot be heard, it has no aroma, and it consists of an immaterial substance. It can be sensed, however, if your sensory perception is strong enough, or has been trained to receive it, which does take a little time.

It is akin to the ether that supports the planets of the universe; it is materialistic yet immaterial, it is substantial as well as being insubstantial. It is as old as the universe that we live in, yet it is as young as a new-born child.

It can be unresisting, yet, at the same time, pliability itself; it weighs nothing yet it cannot be lifted. It is as soft and gentle as a morning breeze, yet it is also a tornado. It is a dew drop, yet it is a tidal wave.

It is life, and the centre of life, for all humanity was born around it. It came into being while you were still in your mother's womb, and it will only leave you when you take in your last breath.

Have you ever had a small baby grip your finger? And did you ever wonder about how strong that hold felt to you? You may even have commented on it at the time, but did you ever consider it beyond that? A newborn baby has had no opportunity to build or develop its muscles, so that tight grip can not be attributed to physical strength. Then what explains this simple phenomenon? The answer is Inner Power.

Another example of this occurred not long ago when a woman started to reverse her car (a Mini) out of her garage. Suddenly she heard a frightful scream. She stopped, leapt out of the car, and almost at once, she saw with horror that her baby was trapped under the rear wheel of her car.

In that split second, probably due to shock, she did an unusual thing. Instead of getting back into the car and driving it forward, or even letting off the handbrake and pushing it forward, she just grabbed the rear bumper and in sheer desperation not only lifted the car off the baby, but also moved the vehicle some nine or ten inches (22 to 24cm) sideways.

She then gently lifted her child into the car and drove straight to the nearest hospital, where fortunately it was found that her little boy was not hurt, apart from a few lacerations and some bruising.

A few days later, after recovering from the shock, she tried to prove to her husband how she had performed that Herculean act — but she could hardly move the body of the car, let alone lift the wheels off the ground. She was a woman of ordinary strength, yet in a few seconds she had found fantastic and unbelievable muscular-force. Her natural Inner Power had come to her aid when she really needed it.

There are many more examples of this kind and perhaps in your own lifetime you may have seen or heard of feats being enacted, which, at the time, did not seem possible. Now you know such things are feasible. For instance, consider the enormous strength and energy displayed by someone out of control, such as a drunken man or a mentally ill person. Inner Power is developed within such a short space of time that even six men might find it difficult to hold somebody during one of these sessions.

Over the years, one wonderful experience has always stood out in my memory. It is a particular demonstration given sometimes by my master, Chan Kam Lee. A lighted candle would be placed on a tall object — such as a table — and this would be positioned a few inches away from a brick wall. My master would then go to the other side of the wall, opposite the candle, and throw a punch at the wall, stopping his fist a short distance from the brickwork. The tremendous force of Inner Power that he generated flowed through his body and down his arm, came out from the front of his fist, penetrated through the wall, and snuffed out the flame of that candle.

You might think that perhaps a trick was involved, but I can personally guarantee that it was absolutely authentic: on a number of occasions I held that lighted candle in my hands myself when this demonstration was given.

What may amaze you even more is the fact that Inner Power is within you, even now as you read this. It is something that is very personal to everyone, because it is an integral part of the body. You were born with it, and it will remain with you until you die. However, when you were about five or six years old, you started to use your physical strength (muscular force) more and more, and your Inner Power less and less, so eventually it became lazy from lack of use, and its potential slowly declined.

Because it has been inactive for so long, when you join any section of the Chinese arts within our Association, our first objective is to help you revive it. Initially there are a few obstacles that have to be overcome, and these are all within yourself, so only you can conquer them and open up the restrictions that have taken effect over the past years. Then, when your Inner Power starts to flow again, you can spend your time learning to cultivate it so that it becomes stronger and stronger as you progress.

In our Association we practise many of the Taoist martial and cultural arts, and we have the largest contingent of practitioners under controlled instruction outside of China.

It is amazing to see young women throwing four and six men simultaneously in the Breath Art (Ch'i Shu); small and weak people punching with the power of ten men in the Boxing Art (Feng Shou kung fu) within two years of training; and people who suffer from all sorts of ill health and sickness, from migraine to arthritis and cancer, becoming healthier and happier in the health arts (Ch'ang Ming). All this and much more is possible through the activation and control of your own Inner Power.

No doubt you are still wondering how it works, and how you can activate it within yourself. The very first principle of gaining Inner Power is to relax (sung) in mind, body and in spirit. This does not mean that you should flop into the nearest armchair and sprawl all over the place, because that type of relaxing means that you are completely giving up all your energy, and in the Chinese arts we call this dying.

We use this period of relaxation to store up energy so that we have that power available whenever we need to use it. However, there are no specific periods when you should relax, for relaxation is something that is innermost within yourself. It is something that you will learn to do whether you are at work or at play, walking, running or sitting down.

Compare yourself to a storage heater: when it is working it is pumping heat into the room, but when it is not doing so — say, for instance, during an off-peak period — then it stores heat within itself to be used at a later time.

This is exactly the same principle by which Inner Power works. We give ourselves time to relax, and we use that period to conserve and store further energy, and as all energy is heat you will readily understand the relationship.

However, because relaxing is slow and arduous, especially in the fast-moving times of modern life, we need something to speed up the process of storing our energy and power, and we require an additional aid to build up the means of generating more heat for our own internal storage heater.

During the first stage in our Chinese arts, relaxation is the hardest objective for the beginner, but while you might feel during the first few months that you are making no progress whatsoever, you should persevere because it takes about nine to twelve months for the average Westerner to feel his Inner Power starting to flow.

Imagine a plastic water pipe. If you squeeze it with your hands or put a kink into it, you will either restrict the flow or stop the water altogether. This is what you do to your own body and mind when you apply stresses and strains upon them.

The first step, therefore, is to throw your whole physical and mental make-up wide open, so that there is not the slightest obstruction anywhere within your system. We know that this is easier said than done, for sometimes you either work too hard or too long, or enjoy the mundane pleasures of life, or you may go to the other extreme by fretting, worrying, or losing your temper. All these daily stresses and strains pound the structure of your physical and mental elements, and cause restrictions and obstructions.

So, the first thing to do to help you relax is collapse your chest and allow your breath (Ch'i) to sink into the abdomen (Tan T'ien). If that sounds complicated then try it another way. Breathe out, and as you do so let your chest and shoulders depress slightly inward and downward as much as you can, but ensure that you keep your back upright.

As you do this you should feel a sensation of the internal weight of the body moving downward and at the same time your abdomen will extend a little. It is best to do this when you are sitting down, either on the floor or on a chair, and then you can feel the sensation of your internal weight moving downward into the lower reaches of the pelvic bone.

Then, as you progress, you will be able to practise the same motions whether you are standing up or even when you are walking. An additional way of speeding up the process of relaxing during your working periods is to take a deep in breath through the nose, and then breathe out through the mouth trying to emulate the above action, anytime during the course of the day. You will rapidly find a marked improvement within yourself, and your health will certainly benefit from it. Better still, make a point of going on to the Taoist Long Life health diet (Ch'ang Ming) and your speed of advancement will surprise you.

In all Association clubs who practise our art of Feng Shou many specialized breathing exercises are included in the training programme, generally at the beginning, middle and the end of the session, which helps every practitioner to get over the first stage.

The second stage along the pathway of developing your Inner Power is known as the propelled movement period, when the trainee learns to direct and control his Inner Power from his lower abdomen to any part of his own body.

If you turn on a valve, you know that you can make the water flow along the pipe, without having to activate the pipe. You can switch on an electrical connection and know that the electricity will flow along the wires, without having to move the wires in the process. Now you can emulate the pipe and the electric wire, for your tissues can carry your inner power to any part of your body without any physical movement whatsoever. In other words, you do not need a single ounce of physical or muscular energy or strength to help the flow of your Inner Power. As a matter of fact, big or tense muscles generally have a tendency to restrict the flow rather than aid it.

We have ways of proving the flow and the degree of its power from any of our students. Proving tests are held at regular intervals so that we can estimate the rate of their progression. There can be no time limits for this stage as it is entirely up to each individual, but on a broad basis it could be anything from one to fifty years, and, in some cases, perhaps never.

One trainee who has been practising one of our Taoist arts for many years, yet has still not yet mastered the first stage because of his attitude, mental tension, and his constant use of physical strength. Unless he learns to conquer himself, starts to relax inwardly, and really makes a conscious effort, he will never accomplish the first stage of gaining mastery of his Inner Power and, most of all, he will never become a master of himself.

The third stage is the level of occlusion, which is the most advanced period of all, and is within reach of everyone provided you are willing to give yourself sufficient time. If you have the mental aptitude you could easily attain the beginnings of this stage within five to six years, but you must be patient and dedicated.

We have mentioned that Inner Power is a kind of heat, and that you can propel it to any part of the body at will. Your abdomen, like the storage heater, has only a limited space or capacity, and sooner or later it will overflow. Other specialized Taoist breathing exercises will help to speed up this overflowing action, and in doing so your abdomen creates more heat.

This overflow will initially fall into the lower extremities of the pelvic bone and the lowest part of the spinal vertebrae. Then, slowly, as the overflowing action continues, Inner Power will gradually seep, of its own accord, through the muscles, tendons and sinews of the body, giving them added strength and still more flexibility and pliability.

Since the bones of the body are sealed units, this makes penetration of Inner Power a little harder and slower, but it can and does penetrate to the innermost parts of the bones, and it does this by a process which is known as osmosis.

Without becoming too technical we will try to explain this to you. As the muscles, tendons and sinews become heated, that heat is passed on to the surface of the bone, and as these are all close to one another, that heat is eventually passed to the bone itself. Then the bone is slowly heated all the way through, and it, in turn, transmits the heat to the marrow which is on the inside of the bone, so that it becomes tempered in the process by a sweating action that takes place. This tempering will make the bone and the marrow as tough as steel, yet within themselves they are more supple than ever before.

Once this unification has taken place, you will have reached the ultimate level of mastery and control of your Inner Power, and thus you will have reached the stage of rejuvenation, when you are able to ward off disease and prolong your life.

To sum up, there is an old Chinese proverb which conveys everything in one simple sentence: 'Old age is inevitable but there is no excuse for senility'. This applies to all of us, whether we be young or old, male or female. Many of the old sages of China proved that by eating and drinking sensibly the Ch'ang Ming way, and developing their Inner Power to a very high level, they were able to live from 150 to 200 years of age.

Now all this may sound fantastic, and you may find it difficult to believe. You may have trouble believing the feats performed by Feng Shou kung fu students and teachers. Anyone who doubts their credibility need only visit any one of the many clubs that are affiliated to our Association to see these feats being performed.

The Taoist Cultural Arts Association

The Lee Family

The history of the Taoist arts within the Lee family goes back over 2,000 years in the town of Wei Hei Wei, on the coast of Central China, about 200 miles from Beijing. The Lee family kept the Taoist arts completely within their own family group for all these years, handing them down from father to son and daughter in an unbroken chain until the early 1930s when Chan Kam Lee, a business man and a native of mainland China, became the last in line of the family to inherit this style.

Chan Kam Lee, was an importer and exporter of precious and semi-precious stones, and therefore had quite a lot of travelling to do especially between Hong Kong, Japan, Singapore and England. Eventually, he set up his main office in London, and in 1930, to find an outlet for his physical, mental and spiritual needs, he opened a small select club in a schoolroom in Red Lion Square, Holborn, Central London, catering for his personal friends and their sons. The total number of students never exceeded a dozen, and as most of them travelled in the course of their business the average attendance was only about six members.

Chee Soo

Chee Soo was born of a Chinese father and an English mother, and as they died when he was only a child, he was brought up by Dr Barnardo's Homes, which is a charitable orphanage. He started his first job as a pageboy in a nursing home in Earl's Court, West London, and he used to go to Hyde Park in his spare time to enjoy the air in the park, watch the horse riders, and to play with his ball, whenever the weather permitted. One Sunday, his ball accidentally hit the back of an old gentleman who was sitting on a park bench. After he had recovered his ball, Chee Soo went up to the gentleman to apologize, only to see that the man was also Chinese. As it was a very rare thing to see another Chinese person in London in those days, the two began to talk together, and arranged to meet again. Whenever the opportunity permitted, the two began to meet regularly and a strong friendship developed between Chee Soo, and the gentleman who was Chan Kam Lee.

In the summer of 1934, Chee Soo was invited to Chan Lee's club, and that is how Chee Soo came to take up the vast range of Taoist martial, philosophical, healing and the cultural arts. In 1939 Chee Soo fought in the war as a Tank Commander in the 2nd Battalion of the Royal Tank Regiment in France, North Africa and Burma, where he was captured by the Japanese. Three years later he finally managed to escape into the Shan Mountains, West Burma, and after a month on the run, threading his way through dense jungle and over the mountains, he eventually made contact with the allies again.

In 1950, Chee Soo, with Chan Lee's permission, formed his own club in Manor Road School, West Ham, East London, where he was living at the time.

Taoist Cultural Arts Association

Chan Lee died in the winter of 1953-4, when his boat sank in a fierce storm off the coast of China, and it was then that his nephew Chee Soo was asked to take over the Presidency of all the Taoist Arts that were being taught. In 1958, Chee Soo set up coaching classes with the object of training qualified teachers, and county, area and regional coaches. Over the years these have proved very successful and there are now classes and clubs operating in many parts of the world, besides those that exist in the British Isles.

Our Association only teaches the Taoist Health arts of The Eight Strands of the Brocade', which comprise:

Ch'ang Ming	—	Taoist Long Life Dietary HealthTherapy
Ts'ao Yao	—	Taoist Herbal Therapy
An Mo	—	Taoist Massage
Tao Yin	—	Taoist Respiration Therapy
Tien Chen	—	Taoist Spot Pressing (Acupressure)
Ch'ili Nung	—	Ch'i, Li, Vibration and Palm Healing
Chen Tuan	—	Taoist Diagnosis Techniques

The Taoist Cultural Arts which comprise:

K'ai Men	—	Taoist Yoga (Chi Kung)
I Fu Shou	—	Sticky or Adhering Hands
Li Kung	—	Taoist development of Li energy
Mo Kun	—	Taoist Wand — external energy control
Mo Hsiang	—	Taoist Meditation

Also:
T'ai Chi Sword, T'ai Chi Stick, T'ai Chi Silk and T'ai Chi Dance.

And the Taoist Self-defence Arts which comprise:
Feng Shou — 'Hand of the Wind' Kung fu, soft and gentle but very fast, and suitable for all age groups.
Chi Shu — Taoist form of Aikido

and all the other forms of the Taoist fighting arts including such weapons as sticks, flails, swords and chopsticks.

Needless to say, all three Arts go together, and all strictly maintain the traditions that were laid down by Chan Kam Lee and his family. Chee Soo, was naturally also a Taoist, and his whole life was dedicated to serving the sick and suffering, and to helping humanity whenever possible. Anyone who is interested in any of these arts can attend the student classes which are held regularly in the British Isles and on the Continent. Weekend courses are also held, together with workshops at Easter and Christmas and in the Summer.

Sadly Chee Soo passed away in 1994 and Marilyn his wife accepted the role of President of the Association at that time.

With her permission the Taoist Cultural Arts Association was formed to carry on the traditions of the Lee family and it's members have dedicated themselves to continue teaching the Taoist Arts in exactly the way they have been passed down to them from Chee Soo himself with nothing added and nothing omitted.

To this end Marilyn kindly entrusted to us the copyright for all Chee Soo's written works regarding the Taoist Arts and it has been our pleasure to re-print these remarkable books and bring out new works which have never before seen the light of day. If you are interested in the Taoist Arts you can find more details on our website at:

www.seahorsearts.co.uk

The Taoist Cultural Arts Association Badge

The outer circle on which is imposed the words 'Taoist Cultural Arts Association', and which is coloured yellow, represents the TAO, which is the Will of the Supreme Spirit, from which all things are created.

The inside black line which separates it from the Yin and Yang represents the Universe, which came into being when the Tao exercised its universal laws, and substance came into being from the chaos of the void.

The Yin and Yang represents the duality of everything within the universe, and nothing can be totally one, for there is always a part of the other within it. It also represents the two sides of the Tao, and the duality within Heaven.

The seahorse is the emblem of the Lee family, and is being carried on by Chee Soo who had Chan Lee's permission to do so. The seahorse is the only mammal where the male takes the newly born children to rear in his pouch. When they are old enough to leave his pouch he dies. In other words, he gives his life for his children.

Index